737
Boeing's Baby

ABOVE • AIRTEAMIMAGES/
MATTHIEU DOUHAIRE

I f you've travelled with a commercial airline on an intra-continental route in the past ten years, you've probably flown on a Boeing 737. Since the type's first flight in April 1967, Boeing's production facility at Renton, Washington has built over 10,000 737 aircraft, with thousands of orders still to be fulfilled. Four generations of the aircraft have served or continue to serve many of the world's leading airlines. Today, a couple of 737 operators are two of the world's best known carriers; Ryanair based in Dublin, Ireland and Southwest Airlines based in Dallas, Texas. Both are low-cost carriers with massive market share in the European and North American market, respectively. Both airlines operate hundreds of aircraft, all of them Boeing 737s. Given its seating capacity, suitability to inter-city routes and a low operating cost base, airlines like the 737.

Passenger opinions on the other hand are less than fixed right now. Fatal crashes of two fourth-generation 737 MAX 8 aircraft in October 2018 and March 2019 which claimed the lives of 346 deaths has tarnished the type's credentials.

But the 737 is not just a commercial jet. Admirals, sailors, generals, and airmen also fly on highly-modified military variants of the 737 in roles as straightforward as cargo airlift to the more specialised radar control and maritime surveillance missions.

Whatever your interest in aviation, 737: Boeing's Baby is packed full of features about legacy and current commercial variants, including extensive content on the 737 MAX, and the big three military types; C-40 Clipper, E-7 Wedgetail and P-8 Poseidon.

Mark Ayton
Editor

CONTENTS

BOEING

Contents

BOEING

BOEING

Editor: Mark Ayton
Senior editor, specials: Roger Mortimer
Email: roger.mortimer@keypublishing.com
Design: Ros Woodham and Lynne Clark
Cover: Steve Donovan
Cover image: AirTeamImages/John Kilmer
Commercial Sales Manager: Andy Mason
Email: Andrew.mason@keypublishing.com
Advertising Production: Rebecca Antoniades
Email: rebecca.antoniades@keypublishing.com

SUBSCRIPTION/MAIL ORDER
Key Publishing Ltd, PO Box 300,
Stamford, Lincs, PE9 1NA
Tel: 01780 480404 **Fax:** 01780 757812
Subscriptions email: subs@keypublishing.com
Mail Order email: orders@keypublishing.com
Website: www.keypublishing.com/shop

PUBLISHING
Group CEO: Adrian Cox
Publisher: Mark Elliott
Head of publishing: Finbarr O'Reilly
Chief Publishing Officer: Jonathan Jackson
Key Publishing Ltd, PO Box 100, Stamford, Lincs, PE9 1XP
Tel: 01780 755131 **Website:** www.keypublishing.com

PRINTING: Precision Colour Printing Ltd, Haldane,
Halesfield 1, Telford, Shropshire. TF7 4QQ

DISTRIBUTION
Seymour Distribution Ltd, 2 Poultry Avenue,
London, EC1A 9PU Enquiries Line: 02074 294000.

BOEING

ROYAL AUSTRALIAN AIR
FORCE/FLT SGT MICK BOTT

Boeing 737
Originals

Mark Broadbent outlines the first variants in the 737 line.

Boeing produced only 30 737-100s and the only extant example is the prototype, N73700 (c/n 19437), now displayed in the Museum of Flight, Seattle. It spent 30 years at the NASA Langley Research Center as Flying Laboratory, registered N515NA, until its retirement on September 27, 2003.

ABOVE • *The first Boeing 737-200 on a test flight.* BOEING

Boeing started to develop a new short-haul airliner to complement their 727 in spring 1964. Preliminary design work resulted in a small twin-jet using the 707's fuselage cross-section and nose with podded engines on the aft fuselage and a T-tail.

Lead engineer Joe Sutter changed this initial configuration. The engines were instead mounted directly to the underside of the wings without pylons and the horizontal stabiliser joined to the aft fuselage, which shortened the landing gear and lowered the fuselage.

This created a 148in-wide fuselage cross-section and comparable capacity with other short-range aircraft of the time such as the original 90-seat Douglas DC-9 Series 10, the BAC One-Eleven 200 (89 seats) and the Sud Aviation SE 210 Caravelle (80 seats). The 14,500lb-thrust Pratt & Whitney JT8D low-bypass ratio turbofan engine was chosen for the new jet.

Development

With an initial programme go-ahead in November 1964 and formal approval by Boeing's board on February 1, 1965, Boeing launched the 737 with an order from Lufthansa for 22 aircraft.

United Airlines was interested but wanted more seats. Responding to the carrier's request, Boeing stretched the 737-100's 94ft-long fuselage to 100ft 2in and increased capacity to 130 seats. This longer-fuselage version was designated the 737-200 and United ordered it.

Both variants were developed simultaneously. The first 737-100 rolled out on January 17, 1967 and flew on April 9, 1967, with the initial 737-200 rolled out on June 29, 1967 and flying on August 8, 1967.

Federal Aviation Administration type certification for the two versions followed on December 15, 1967 and 13 days later the first 737-100 was delivered to Lufthansa. The German carrier put it into service on February 10, 1968, with United's inaugural 737-200 flight on April 28, 1968.

Early Improvements

The 737-100 and 737-200 were the only 737 variants to feature aft airstairs, mounted on a special aft entry door in the rear fuselage.

Airlines' preference for the higher-capacity 737-200 was apparent quickly – apart from Lufthansa the only other customers for the 737-100 were Malaysia Airlines (five) and Avianca (two). Still, with flight testing showing greater-than-anticipated drag, Boeing realised its new aircraft could be improved.

The original clamshell thrust reversers were replaced by hydraulically powered target-style reversers to improve short-field performance, with thrust deflected inboard over the wings and outboard under the wings. Boeing received

FAA certification for these changes on February 20, 1969. Retrofits were provided for delivered aircraft.

737-200 Advanced

Boeing launched a high gross weight variant of the 737-200 in 1971 called the 737-200 Advanced, which made the new thrust reversers standard. Other improvements were introduced including larger leading-edge flaps, redesigned slats and engine nacelles and wider engine pylons to improve aerodynamics and create better short-field performance, automatic wheel brakes, greater fuel capacity, uprated Pratt & Whitney (P&W) JT8D-15 engines and a higher maximum take-off weight.

The 737-200 Advanced first flew on April 15, 1971, with FAA certification and service entry with All Nippon Airways following a month later. The variant became the production standard 737 in June 1971, with retrofits made available for existing operators.

These were not the last modifications for the early 737. As aircraft noise became a more pressing issue during the 1970s, the nacelle was acoustically lined by Boeing and P&W swapped one fan stage for two compressor stages to reduce noise. Quebecair was the first to introduce this 'quiet' nacelle configuration.

Boeing also introduced a gravel kit to enable operations from unprepared runways. This included a deflection ski on the nose gear to keep gravel off the underbelly, deflectors on the main gear to prevent damage to the flaps, protective shields for tubing and cables, glass fibre-reinforced flaps,

Teflon for wing and fuselage surfaces, a retractable anti-collision light, and strengthened aerials. The kit also featured a small forward projecting tube blowing bleed air over the engine nacelles to break up vortices that could ingest gravel.

Combi

Boeing launched a combi variant of the 737-200 Advanced able to transport both passengers and freight, the 737-200C/737-200QC (Quick Change) on September 18, 1968.

The combi aircraft had a 138 x 86in side cargo door on the forward port side to load pallets. With strengthened floors and additional seat tracks to accommodate seven 88 x 125in pallets on the main deck, a moveable partition enabled seats to be added or removed based on passenger numbers and freight loads.

The crew were able to pressurise or depressurise the passenger compartment for smoke clearance. The changeover time was approximately three hours on the 737-200C and one hour on the 737-200QC.

Air Alaska was a notable 737-200QC

ABOVE LEFT • *The first Boeing 737-100 during its maiden flight.* BOEING

ABOVE RIGHT • *The initial 737-100 spent 30 years at the NASA Langley Research Center.* NASA

BELOW • *Only around 50 737-200s still fly including this Nolinor aircraft in Canada.* AIRTEAMIMAGES/MATTHIEU POULIOT

LEFT • *A 737-200 landing gear with its Gravel Deflector device.* BOEING

This aircraft was used in numerous research projects including electronic flight displays, precision flare control, surface coatings to improve laminar flow, digital communications, precision guidance, energy control systems, take-off performance, data links, GPS systems, and engine monitoring and control.

Still Flying

Boeing built 1,114 737-200s, delivering the last 737-200 Advanced (c/n 24236) to Xiamen Airlines in August 1988.

At the time of writing in November 2020, around 50 737-200s still fly worldwide. Most are in the developing world, with operators such as Avior Airlines, ConVasia and RUTACA in Venezuela, Chilean Airways, Mineral Airways in Peru, and Aviatsa in Honduras. Military 737-200s are active in Bolivia, the Democratic Republic of Congo, Ecuador, and Indonesia.

Combi-configured examples operate on passenger and cargo routes in Canada thanks to operators Air Inuit (four examples), Canadian North (two) and Nolinor (eight).

operator, using nine examples from 1981 to operate onto ice runways at remote airports in northern Canada.

NASA Test Aircraft

Boeing produced only 30 737-100s and the only extant 737-100 is the prototype, N73700 (c/n 19437), now displayed in the Museum of Flight, Seattle. It spent 30 years at the NASA Langley Research Center as Flying Laboratory N515NA until its retirement on September 27, 2003.

737 Originals Characteristics

	737-100	737-200
Length	94ft	100ft 2in
Height	36ft	36ft
Wingspan	93ft	93ft
Max take-off weight	Up to 110,000lb	Up to 128,100lb
Max landing weight	Up to 99,000lb	Up to 107,000lb
Max zero fuel weight	Up to 90,000lb	Up to 95,000lb
Operating empty weight	TBD	
Max structural payload	Up to 28,000lb	Up to 35,200lb
Useable fuel	Up to 4,720 US gal	Up to 4,780 US gal
Engines	2x Pratt & Whitney JT8D	2x Pratt & Whitney JT8D
Max speed	Mach 0.74-Mach 0.82	Mach 0.74-Mach 0.82
Ceiling	37,000ft	37,000ft
Range	1,540nm	2,600nm
Seats	85 two-class	102 two-class

Source: Boeing 737 Characteristics for Airport Planning

Boeing 737
Classics

New engines, more capacity and longer range were introduced with the 737-300, 737-400 and 737-500, as **Mark Broadbent** explains.

By the late 1970s, with McDonnell Douglas evolving its single-aisle airliner with the MD-80 series, Boeing wanted to increase the 737's capacity, extend range and improve performance. Development began in 1979 and the result was the addition of three second-generation versions of the aircraft: the 737-300, 737-400 and 737-500.

The 737-300 was first to be developed. It took its maiden flight on February 24, 1984, entering service with USAir on November 24 that year following certification earlier in the month.

The stretched 737-400, designed to complement the 737-300 and the larger 757-200, flew on February 19, 1988 and entered service on September 15 of the same year with Piedmont Airlines. The shortened 737-500, designed to replace the 737-200, was launched in 1987. It flew on June 30, 1989 and entered service with Southwest Airlines on February 28, 1990.

From P&W to CFM

For the second-generation 737, Boeing chose to re-engine the aircraft with CFM International CFM56 turbofans to reduce fuel burn and noise.

The 737's low ground clearance, a trait from the original 707-derived fuselage, meant CFM engineers had to reduce the CFM56's fan diameter and bypass ratio and reposition the accessory gearbox, resulting in the distinctive flat-bottomed shape of the air intake on the engines.

The CFM56s were also mounted forward of the wing struts instead of tucked directly beneath the wing, as on the original versions. The wings were extended by nine inches to 94ft 9in using tip extensions and strengthened to accommodate a higher gross weight. Trailing-edge slats and flaps were adjusted and strengthened tyres, wheels and brakes introduced.

A substantial number of replaceable parts were identical to those on the 737-200 to give operators simplified spares inventories and maintenance requirements. The 737-300, 737-400 and 737-500 were also designed to have the same handling characteristics as the 737-200 to enable a shared type rating to fly all the models of them.

Three Different Variants

At 109ft 7in in length the 737-300 is 9ft 5in longer than the 737-200, enabling it to seat 126 passengers in a typical two-class layout (or a maximum 149 single-class). Powered

by the CFM56-3C1, the aircraft offers up to 2,255nm range, a cruise speed of Mach 0.78 and up to 138,500lb maximum take-off weight (MTOW).

A further 10ft fuselage stretch of the 737-399 created the 119ft 7in-long 737-400, seating 147 passengers two-class or 159 one-class. This variant was also powered by an uprated 23,500lb CFM56-3C1, but its greater length required a ventral skid to prevent tailstrike damage due to over-rotation, two extra over-wing exits and an upgraded air-conditioning system. Its standard MTOW is 150,000lb.

Designed to succeed the 737-200, the third and final Classic variant was the shortened 101ft 9in-long 737-500, powered by 20,100lb-rated (89.4kN) CFM56-3C1s and offering 2,375nm range and a 133,500lb MTOW.

Orders

Customers for the 737-300, 737-400 and 737-500 spanned major network players, small national airlines, and charter carriers.

By the early 1990s the rising market share of the fly-by-wire Airbus A320, the European manufacturer's first single-aisle narrowbody airliner, meant Boeing had to update the 737 again. The result was the re-winged, updated, more efficient 737 Next Generation models, the arrival of which meant the 737-300, 737-400 and 737-500 were dubbed 737 Classics.

Despite the new variants arriving, the 737 Classic's order backlog meant production continued for a while. Although the first 737NG variant entered service early in 1998, the last new-build 737-500 (JA307K c/n 29795) was only delivered to Air Nippon on July 21, 1999, followed by the last 737-300 (ZK-NGJ c/n 25609) to Air New Zealand on December 17, 1999 and the final 737-400 (OK-FGS c/n 28478) to CSA Czech Airlines on February 25, 2000.

According to Boeing's orders and deliveries data, the company produced 1,988 737 Classics, comprising 1,113 737-300s, 486 737-400s and 389 737-500s. These aircraft gave the 737 its place as the biggest-selling airliner ever developed.

Continued Operations

The operational 737 Classic population has diminished in size over the past decade as newer and more efficient aircraft arrive. Southwest, which operated more examples than any other

ABOVE • *Klasjet 737-500 LY-JMS (c/n 26680) shows the flat-bottomed CFM International CFM56 engines that distinguish the 737 Classics.*

737 Classics Characteristics

	737-300	737-400	737-500
Length	109ft 7in	119ft 7in	101ft 9in
Height	36ft 4in	36ft 4in	36ft 4in
Wingspan	94ft 9in	94ft 9in	94ft 9in
Max take-off weight	135,000lb with CFM56-3B1 or 139,500lb with CFM56-3B2	150,000lb	133,500lb with CFM56-3B1 or 136,000lb with CFM56-3B2
Max landing weight	114,000lb with CFM56-3B1 or 116,600lb with CFM56-3B2	124,000lb	110,000lb
Max zero fuel weight	106,500lb with CFM56-3B1 or 109,600lb with CFM56-3B2	117,000lb	102,500lb with CFM56-3B1 or 103,000lb with CFM56-3B2
Max structural payload	35,600lb with CFM56-3B1 or 33,960lb with CFM56-3B2	43,830lb	33,470lb
Useable fuel	Up to 6,295 US gal if using auxiliary tanks	Up to 6,295 US gal if using auxiliary tanks	Up to 6,295 US gal if using auxiliary tanks
Engines (initial variant)	2x CFM International CFM56-3B1s	2x CFM International CFM56-3B1s	2x CFM International CFM56-3B1s
Max cruise speed	Mach 0.74	Mach 0.74	Mach 0.74
Ceiling	37,000ft	37,000ft	37,000ft
Range	2,255nm	2,060nm	2,375nm
Seats	128 two-class	146 two-class	108 two-class

Source: Boeing 737 Characteristics for Airport Planning

carrier, phased out the 737-300 in 2017 and AirBaltic, All Nippon Airways, LOT Polish Airlines, Lufthansa and Norwegian are other carriers to have said farewell to different 737 Classic variants.

Older aircraft may perform less efficiently but they do have low ownership costs, making them attractive to smaller operators in secondary markets. Such operators include Air Nauru (four 737-300s including the last 737-300 delivered, now registered VH-NXU), Boliviana (nine 737-300s), Belavia (four 737-300s) and Smartavia (three 737-500s)

And despite the young blood of BBJs, some 737 Classics still fly as bizjets. Indeed, aircraft with favourable flying hours, maintenance records and ownership costs continue to receive cabin and equipment upgrades

For example, the 33-year-old 737-300 N444HE (c/n 60393) was at the time of writing in November 2020 listed for sale by the business aviation consulting firm Corporate Concepts International, Inc.

The sales listing described the aircraft as having 'exceptional pedigree'. Purchased new from Boeing in 1987 by Doris Duke (once the wealthiest woman in the United States), the aircraft was later owned by the DeVos family, the founders of Amway. The aircraft's current private owner is described as having 'businesses and homes [in] Los Angeles, Europe, North Africa, the Middle East, and Asia'.

With 7,500 flying hours on the clock N444HE was upgraded early in 2020. The listing said: "The aircraft has been owned by three very high net worth families and nothing has been overlooked or ignored regarding maintenance and upgrades."

The upgrade involved a heavy maintenance check and repaint, the CFM International CFM56s overhauled and retrofitted with new compressor blades featuring improved blade angles to improve fuel efficiency, and an interior refit by Associated Air Center in Dallas, Texas.

'Maybe there's something to the survival of the fittest theory after all' ran a 1995 Boeing advertisement promoting its 737 Next Generation (737NG) airliners. The advert linked the new version with the sales success of the older 737 variants.

Today, with over 6,000 Boeing 737-600, 737-700, 737-800 and 737-900 family aircraft and derivatives built, the 737NG has ensured the 737's place as one of the most successful commercial airliners of all time.

Origins

Boeing had dominated the short-medium haul twinjet market with the 737 since the 1960s, but the Airbus A320's success meant the company had to respond.

From 1991 Boeing examined several options, including producing an all-new aircraft, but decided on developing new versions of the 737. It felt developing a proven design with new technology would be more attractive in a time of economic turbulence, while also offering operational commonality for existing customers.

Originally known as the 737-X, the Boeing 737 Next Generation comprised

Next
Generation

The 737-600, 737-700, 737-800 and 737-900 launched in the 1990s were the third generation 737 models. **Mark Broadbent** outlines the different models and their evolution over the years.

ABOVE • *A landing 737-900ER in Boeing's 2000s white and blue colours.* BOEING

four new 737 variants of differing fuselage lengths – the 737-600, 737-700, 737-800 and 737-900.

A new supercritical wing, tail section and stabiliser was designed for the 737NG. The new wing is 16ft (4.88m) wider and 25% larger in area than the wing on the 737 Classic series aircraft (737-300, 737-400 and 737-500), which increased the 737's fuel capacity by 30%

and aerodynamic efficiency by 22%.

The CFM International CFM56-7 was selected to power the new models. With full authority digital engine control (FADEC) software used to optimise thrust, and larger exhaust ducts and nacelles, the 737NG was also 12 decibels quieter and 7% more fuel efficient than the 737 Classic.

The flight deck was redesigned, and a completely new interior cabin

used the curved ceiling and rounded overhead bins from the Boeing 777. Taking advantage of the great strides in computing in the 1990s, the 737NG was the first Boeing aircraft to be designed fully by digital design software.

Variants

The 737NG was formally launched on November 17, 1993, with Southwest

Airlines the launch customer. The four new 737NG variants were all developed concurrently, but the 737-700 was the first of the new family to appear.

The prototype rolled out at Seattle, Washington, on December 8, 1996 and made its first flight on February 9, 1997. Following US Federal Aviation Administration certification on November 7, 1997, Southwest undertook the first 737-700 revenue flights on January 18, 1998.

Designed to replace the 737-300, the 737-700 can seat up to 141 passengers two-class or 149 in all-economy. It has a range of 3,010nm, a cruise speed of Mach 0.78 and a maximum take-off weight of up to 153,000lb.

Next to follow was the 737-800, a stretched version of the 737-700 designed to succeed the 737-400. It first flew on July 31, 1997, was certified on March 13, 1998, and entered service with Hapag-Lloyd Airlines (now TUIfly) on April 24, 1998.

The 737-800 is 129ft 6in long thanks to the addition of fuselage 'plugs' forward and aft of the wings. The greater length means it carries up to 189 passengers

> With over 6,000 Boeing 737-600, 737-700, 737-800 and 737-900 family aircraft and derivatives built, the 737 Next Generation has ensured the 737's place as one of the most successful commercial airliners of all time.

one-class and 178 two-class.

Although it has shorter range than the 737-700, it has a higher maximum take-off weight of 174,200lb. Its larger size means its CFM56s have more thrust than those on the 737-700 and, to account for the greater capacity, additional over-wing exits, 'up-gauged' fuselage stringers and skins, a tailskid, and heavier-duty landing gear, wheels, and brakes.

The third variant to be developed was the 737-600. Essentially a shortened version of the 737-700, the 737-600 is 102ft 6in long and features derated CFM56s. Designed to succeed the 737-500, it seats 130 passengers in a one-class layout. Its maximum take-off weight is 145,500lb, some 12,000lb more than its predecessor. It first flew on January 22, 1998 and entered service with launch customer SAS on

October 25 that year.

The fourth 737NG family member is the 737-900, launched in 1997 with an order from Alaska Airlines. Following a maiden flight on August 3, 2000, it entered service on May 25, 2001. At 138ft 2in in length, the 737-900 was the longest 737 at the time, with room for 220 passengers in an all-economy layout. Its extra length comes from a 54in section fore of the wing and a 42in section aft of the wing, with the aircraft having a higher maximum take-off weight of 187,700lb.

Longer-range derivatives of some 737NG variants followed. The 737-900ER (Extended Range) was launched in July 2005. Although it has the same fuselage length as the 737-900, the 737-900ER has a flat aft pressure bulkhead, providing room for an extra fuselage frame. This increased capacity to 215

ABOVE • *UTair has received ten 737-800s.* BOEING

BELOW • *Many low-cost carriers such as Jet2 expanded using 737NGs.* BOEING

Developed concurrently with the 737-900 was the 737-700ER. This variant, essentially a commercial passenger version of the BBJ1 (itself a derivative of the 737-700) combines the 737-700's fuselage with the 737-800's wings and landing gear. The first customer delivery was to All Nippon Airways on February 16, 2007.

A further derivative of the basic 737NG models was the 737-700C, a convertible version of the 737-700. The seats in this aircraft can be removed to carry cargo, which is loaded through a door on the port side. It can seat 148 passengers in a one-class seating arrangement and lift to 38,700lb payloads.

and later 737 Classics, delivered to a customer either with a Boeing-supplied interior or 'green' (no paint or interior) for a third-party specialist to install a customised interior at a completion centre of the customer's choosing.

But the 737 as a bizjet stepped into a different league in the 1990s when the Boeing Business Jet (BBJ) variants of the 737NG models were developed.

First up was the BBJ, a variant of the 737-700 launched on July 2, 1996, rolled out on July 26, 1998, and first flown on September 4, 1998. It was certified on October 30, 1998 with the first customer delivery following on September 4, 1999.

This was followed by the BBJ2, a variant of the 737-800. Launched in October 1999, production began in September 2000, with the first customer delivery on February 28, 2001. The BBJ 737 product line expanded further in 2006 with the BBJ3, a variant of the 737-900ER (itself a longer-range derivative of the 737-900). It was delivered to its first customer on August 2, 2008.

The BBJ, BBJ2 and BBJ3 types are all, respectively, 737-700/737-800/737-900ER aircraft built and delivered to a customer without any interior furnishings to enable the customer to install their specific cabin configuration.

The most significant difference between a regular airline 737NG and the BBJs are the large auxiliary fuel tanks aboard. The BBJ combines the 737-700's airframe with the strengthened wing, fuselage centre section and landing gear of the larger 737-800, enabling auxiliary fuel tanks to be installed in the belly to give the aircraft long range.

The BBJ auxiliary tank fuel system was ✈

RIGHT • *One of the 100 737-800s delivered to Air China.* BOEING

BOTTOM RIGHT • *A 737-800 in Boeing's 1990s red, white and blue livery.* BOEING

passengers in an all-economy layout compared to the 737-900's 189 seats. Range was extended to 3,265nm with the addition of two auxiliary fuel tanks.

The 737-900's flight test programme began on September 1, 2006, with FAA certification following on April 26, 2007 and the first aircraft was delivered to launch operator Lion Air the following day.

Bizjets

These models provided the basis for more derivatives, notably business jet (bizjet) variants.

Boeing had long offered these variants, launching the 737-200 Executive (originally designated the Corporate 77-32 or the Corporate 200) in 1968

737-600 Characteristics

Length	102ft 6in
Height	41ft 3in
Wingspan	112ft 7in (117ft 5in with Blended Winglets)
Max take-off weight	124,000-144,500lb
Max landing weight	120,500-121,500lb
Max zero fuel weight	113,500-114,500lb
Max structural payload	33,300-34,300lb
Useable fuel	6,875 US gal
Engines	2x CFM International CFM56-7Bs
Max cruise speed	Mach 0.78
Ceiling	41,000ft
Range	3,235nm
Seats	108 two-class, 130 all-economy

designed by PATS, Inc, a Georgetown, Delaware-based company acquired in 1999 by DeCrane Aerospace. The auxiliary fuel system for the BBJ was a derivative of the aux tank systems PATS previously developed for 727, 737, 757, 767 and MD-80-series aircraft.

Designed specifically for the BBJ, the system includes supplemental fuel tanks in both the forward and aft cargo holds. The system can accommodate various combinations of forward and aft fuel tanks: from one tank holding 520 additional gallons of fuel to nine tanks holding more than 3,800 additional gallons. Customers select their preferred tank arrangement based on their operational requirements, with tank installation taking place during the completion process.

Different BBJ variants offer varying range depending on the exact passenger configuration. The first BBJ has up to 6,200nm range with eight passengers, 5,980nm with 25 passengers or 5,510nm with 50

passengers. The BBJ2 has up to 5,735nm with 25 passengers or 4,935nm with 50, and the BBJ3 has 5,545nm with up to 50 passengers.

To highlight the BBJ's range capability, in September 2012 an example owned by Samsung Electronics was flown from Los Angeles to Auckland, New Zealand for the first interior completion of a new BBJ by Auckland-based Altitude Aerospace Interiors. The aircraft flew the 5,658 nautical mile trip in 13 hours, seven minutes and 54 seconds, a new world record for 'speed over a recognised course' and landed in Auckland with 7,800lb of fuel remaining.

Boeing Business Jets' president at the time, Steve Taylor, who captained the flight, commented: "When we left Los Angeles with full fuel, we were 21,000lb below our maximum take-off weight. This means that the customer can add a full VIP interior, fill all the seats and still carry full fuel and have remarkable range."

Interiors are produced to the specifications and preferences of

737-700 Characteristics

Length	110ft 4in
Height	41ft 3in
Wingspan	112ft 7in (117ft 5in with Blended Winglets)
Max take-off weight	133,000lb without winglets, 153,000lb with winglets, 154,500lb on 737-700C
Max landing weight	128,000lb with or without winglets, 129,2000lb on 737-700C
Max zero fuel weight	120,500lb with or without winglets, 121,700lb on 737-700C
Max structural payload	37,500lb with or without winglets, 38,700lb on 737-700C
Useable fuel	6,875 US gal
Engines	2x CFM International CFM56-7Bs
Max cruise speed	Mach 0.78
Ceiling	41,000ft
Range	3,010nm
Seats	141 two-class, 149 all-economy

In 2011 Boeing launched the ecoDemonstrator programme to flight-test new technologies to accelerate getting them onto in-production or in-development aircraft. Work on a revised winglet with improved natural laminar flow was the real breakthrough. Measurements taken from the test flights were later used in the design of the 737 MAX's Advanced Technology Winglet.

ABOVE • *Korean Air Lines is one of relatively few 737-900ER operators.* BOEING

RIGHT • *An adaptive trailing edge, new actuators, and a variable area fan nozzle to reduce noise were among technologies tested on an American Airlines 737-800 in the ecoDemonstrator.* BOEING

individual customers. However, typical configuration includes a crew rest area behind the cockpit, a forward lounge, a private suite with bed and private bathroom facilities including shower, and then first class sleeper seats, with a galley and bathroom facilities at the rear of the aircraft. There are also options for meeting and conference areas. The cabins of all the BBJ variants feature a lower cabin altitude of 6,500ft instead of the standard 8,000ft cabin to increase passenger comfort.

According to Boeing's orders and deliveries data, 110 examples of the BBJ variants of the 737NG have been delivered over the last 22 years comprising 78 BBJs, 24 BBJ2s and eight BBJ3s.

Blended Winglets

The BBJs have an important role in the 737 story besides simply being further derivatives of the 737NG models.

As Boeing sought to extract the best performance and furthest range from the aircraft to enable the BBJ to compete effectively with other business jets, along came the distinctive Blended Winglets, the fin-like wingtip devices developed by Aviation Partners Boeing (see Winglets).

First introduced as standard equipment on the BBJ, Blended Winglets are designed to help optimise cruise performance at altitude, reduce

ABOVE LEFT • *Boeing introduced the Sky Interior for the 737NG cabin.* BOEING

LEFT • *The last 737NG to be assembled for airline, for KLM, arrives in Amsterdam in 2019.* KLM ROYAL DUTCH AIRLINES/DESRIL SANTOSO TEGUH

engine maintenance costs and cut the 737NG's noise on take-off. The results they produced meant they subsequently made their way onto the main 737NG models both as a line-fit option on production jets and as a retrofit on aircraft already in service. More than 5,000 are now in use, and virtually every 737NG produced from the early 2000s has received them.

Blended Winglets' introduction to the 737NG reflected how Boeing had to maintain market share in an increasingly intense competition with Airbus. This rivalry, which intensified during the 2000s, means Boeing has

created numerous other performance enhancements for the 737NG family since its debut.

Other Performance Enhancements

While Blended Winglets are the most visually prominent performance improvement made to the initial 737NG, Boeing has also made many other changes to the aircraft over the years, responding to airlines' concerns for fuel efficiency and lower operational costs.

A short-field performance package for all 737NG models (except the 737-900ER) was approved by regulators in 2006,

involving retrofit modifications to slats, flaps and flight management computer software revisions to allow payload increases of 3,750lb for take-off and 10,000lb for landing in 'hot and high' areas.

A retrofit package offering lighter and more efficient carbon brakes for all 737NGs was also launched in 2006, with Delta Air Lines the first customer to order them for its 737-700s two years later.

Avionics improvements included a head-up display; a Quiet Climb System to automatically reduce engine thrust in noise-sensitive areas; a Vertical Situation Display, presenting a side view of the aircraft's flight path relative to terrain; Integrated Approach Navigation, a set of common approach procedures to reduce pilot workload; and an updated GPS Landing System.

A Surface Guidance System, aimed at helping pilots reduce the risk of collision with other aircraft and vehicles whilst taxiing, and Enhanced Vision and Synthetic Vision Systems which respectively present infrared and computer-generated views of the outside world to the pilots, were further avionics changes.

In 2011 Boeing introduced a Performance Improvement Package (PIP) for the 737NG, which introduced streamlined surfaces onto several fairings and controls. The housing for the anti-collision lights, the plug and cutback nozzle on the CFM56 engines and environmental control system exhaust now all have curved rather than angular surfaces.

The aluminium filler formerly used on the slat and spoiler trailing edges was replaced by machine-tapered filler which is 60% thinner. The gaps between the spoilers and respective flaps were reduced by a measure between 0.05and 0.32in depending on the flap. Five aft wheel-well fairings

737-800 Characteristics

Length	129ft 6in
Height	41ft 2in
Wingspan	112ft 7in (117ft 5in with Blended Winglets)
Max take-off weight	Up to 174,200lb with winglets
Max landing weight	Up to 146,300lb with winglets
Max zero fuel weight	Up to 138,300lb with winglets
Max structural payload	Up to 47,000lb with winglets
Useable fuel	6,875 US gal
Engines	2x CFM International CFM56-7Bs
Max cruise speed	Mach 0.78
Ceiling	41,000ft
Range	2,935nm
Seats	178 two-class, 189 all-economy

737-900/737-900ER Characteristics

Length	138ft 2in
Height	41ft 2in
Wingspan	112ft 7in (117ft 5in with Blended Winglets)
Max take-off weight	Up to 174,200lb with winglets, 187,700lb on 737-900ER
Max landing weight	Up to 147,300lb with winglets, 157,300lb on 737-900ER
Max zero fuel weight	Up to 140,300lb with winglets, 149,300lb on 737-900ER
Max structural payload	Up to 45,720lb with winglets, 50,805lb on 737-900ER
Useable fuel	7,390 US gal with winglets, 7,837 US gal on 737-900ER
Engines	2x CFM International CFM56-7Bs
Max cruise speed	Mach 0.78
Ceiling	41,000ft
Range	2,950nm
Seats	193 two-class, 220 all economy

and five panels at the rear of the main undercarriage wheel bay were re-contoured. These changes were all carried out to smooth the airflow around the back of the wing and the gear when it is extended for take-off and landing.

These changes, tested on a United Airlines 737-800 in 2010/2011, may seem minor but operators who opted for the PIP on its release, including Japan Airlines and flyDubai, were by the end of 2012 reporting a 2% reduction in fuel burn. Boeing said the PIP reduces the cost of operating one 737NG by $120,000 per year.

Boeing also developed a revised cabin design, Sky Interior, for the 737NG, with the first aircraft so equipped delivered to flyDubai in October 2010. A version of the cabin design initially developed for the 787, the Sky Interior features curved sidewalls and ceiling, re-shaped window reveals, noise-dampening materials, larger overhead storage bins and programmable LED mood lighting,

ecoDemonstrator

In 2011 Boeing launched the ecoDemonstrator programme to flight-test new technologies to accelerate getting them onto in-production or in-development aircraft.

The ecoDemonstrator programme's first year in 2012 was a collaboration between Boeing, American Airlines, and the US Federal Aviation Administration. American supplied a 737-800, N897NN (c/n 33318) for the test work undertaken at Glasgow, Montana, Reno, Nevada, and Washington, DC.

An adaptive trailing edge, new actuators for the CFM56 engine mounts to cancel vibration, a variable area fan nozzle to reduce noise, a regenerative fuel cell to generate power independently from engine-driven electrical systems, and new flight trajectory software for more efficient routings were among technologies tried out on N897NN.

However, the real breakthrough was work with a revised winglet with improved natural laminar flow (the smoothness of the flow over the airfoil). Measurements taken from the test flights were later used in the design of the 737 MAX's Advanced Technology (AT) Winglet.

Numbers

Boeing's orders and deliveries data shows it sold 4,991 737-800s. The next most popular model is the 737-700 (1,128), followed by the 737-900ER (505). Sixty-nine 737-600s were sold and 52 737-900s.

In the 2010s Boeing ramped up output to meet demand, hiking production from 31.5 units per month in 2010 to 35 in 2012 and then 38 in 2013. Output reached 42 jets a month in 2014 and 47 in 2017, with further increases to 52 and then 57 a month in 2019.

The 737NG orders backlog gradually diminished during the 2010s. Boeing built the last passenger 737NGs in 2019 (production of the military versions continues, of course). The final aircraft for an airline to be assembled was 737-800 PH-BCL (c/n 63624), handed over to KLM Royal Dutch Airlines at Amsterdam Schiphol on December 18, 2019.

Unusually, this last production jet was not the final 737NG delivery – which was the handover to China Eastern Airlines of two 737-800s, B-20A8 (c/n 63088) and B-20A1 (c/n 63087), on January 5, 2020.

ABOVE • *Luxurious interiors are available for all BBJ variants.* BOEING

ABOVE RIGHT • *A typical dining arrangement on a BBJ 737.* BOEING

BELOW • *The extremely well-appointed passenger cabin of a Boeing Business Jet.* BOEING

BELOW RIGHT • *A Boeing Business Jet on take off.* BOEING

ABOVE LEFT • *A United Air Lines 737-800 was used to flight-test a Performance Improvement Package introduced for the 737NG in 2011.* BOEING

LEFT • *Many low-cost carriers such as Ryanair expanded using 737NGs.* BOEING

MAX

Mark Broadbent describes the fourth generation 737 and key technical aspects of the aircraft.

In December 2010 Airbus announced it would re-engine its A320 family, the 737's direct competitor in the single-aisle narrowbody airliner segment. The European builder amassed more than 1,200 orders for the new-generation aircraft within six months.

By mid-2011, the aerospace industry wanted to know how Boeing would respond. During a 2011 Paris Air Show briefing, Boeing Commercial Airplanes' chief executive officer at the time, Jim Albaugh, was non-committal, asking the following rhetorical question: "Do we want to evolve an airplane [the 737] with an incremental increase [in performance] or do we want to take more risk and design an airplane for the next fifty years that really addresses where our customers' needs are?".

Boeing was exploring an all-new narrowbody airliner with its New Small Airplane (NSA) concept studies, and some influential customers wanted a new jet. Steven Udvár-Hazy, CEO of lessor Air Lease said during that Paris event that he was "ready to sit down and make a deal on a new airplane." Norwegian Air Shuttle's CEO Bjorn Kjos urged Boeing to "take the next giant leap," saying there was a "long queue of airlines [waiting to] tell Boeing

they have to build a new aircraft."

Jeffrey Knittel from lessor CIT said, "I would hope [Boeing] will come to a decision soon," and Qatar Airways CEO Akbar Al-Baker quipped that Boeing was "pussy-footing" around the decision.

Re-Engine and New Variants

In the end, Boeing parked the NSA in favour of a re-engine. It formally launched the fourth 737 generation, the 737 MAX, on September 30, 2011.

The 737-700, 737-800 and 737-900ER would be re-engined with CFM International LEAP-1B turbofans to become the 737 MAX 7, 737 MAX 8 and 737 MAX 9, respectively. The 737 MAX 8 would be the baseline version and developed first, with the larger 737 MAX 9 and smaller 737 MAX 7 following later.

The three initial variants of the 737 MAX are each designed for different needs in the short-haul market. The 737 MAX 8 has capacity for 178 passengers two-class or 189 single-class and is designed for operators' key trunk routes.

The 737 MAX 9 seats 193 passengers two-class (or 220 single-class) for operators wanting to add more capacity to popular routes, and the 737 MAX 7 for 138 passengers two-class (156 one-class, 172 maximum) for airlines looking at network development opportunities or range and hot and high requirements.

The smallest 737NG variant, the 737-600, was not part of the re-engine. Mirroring Airbus' choice not to re-engine the A318 on launching the A320neo, Boeing's decision reflected the market's preference for larger-capacity aircraft.

This industry trend for bigger single aisles saw the 737 MAX range further expanding in the years after its launch with new higher-capacity options. The 737 MAX 200, a subvariant of the 737 MAX 8 with 200 seats, was launched on September 8, 2014.

Lengthened Fuselage

Then on June 19, 2017, the year that marked half a century since the 737's first flight, on the opening morning of the 52nd International Paris Air Show at Le Bourget, Boeing formally launched the 737 MAX 10. It was the fourth major variant in the latest generation alongside the 737 MAX 7, 737 MAX 8 and 737 MAX 9.

The 737 MAX 10 is a stretched derivative of the 737 MAX 9. It will have the same 117ft 10in wingspan as all the other 737 MAX family variants but at 143ft 8in in length it will be 66in longer than the 138ft 4in-long 737 MAX 9. The extra length comes from two more fuselage barrels, one 40in barrel fore of the wings and one 26in barrel aft of the wings. Range will be 3,215nm.

The extra length will give two extra rows of seating, meaning the 737 MAX 10 will be able to seat between 230 passengers single-class, or 188 passengers in a two-class layout. This compares to 162 seats one-class in the 737 MAX 8 and 178 seats one-class in the 737 MAX 9, and is up from the maximum 220 seats of the 737 MAX 200 that until the 737 MAX 10's launch was the family member offering most seats.

Changes from the 737 MAX 9 are a variable exit limit rating mid-exit door added to the fuselage, a lighter flat aft pressure bulkhead, a modified wing for low speed drag reduction, a modified landing gear and a slightly modified wing to accommodate the revised gear. The aircraft will be powered by a higher-thrust version of the CFM International LEAP-1B engine that powers all 737 MAX variants.

The landing gear required modification because the 737 MAX 10's slightly extra length of course requires greater ground clearance for when the aircraft rotates or lands. The gear will be 'semi-levered' – a feature first developed in the early 2000s for the 777-300ER. A semi-levered gear shifts the centre of rotation rearwards from the main axle on the main landing gear to the aft axle, which creates the required ground clearance to avoid a tailstrike.

Like its family stablemates the 737 MAX 10 will be powered by CFM International LEAP-1B engines and feature Advanced Technology winglets and the Boeing Sky Interior as standard.

Boosting Capacity

Boeing announced 361 commitments for the 737 MAX 10 during the 2017 Paris launch, comprising firm orders, purchase commitments and memorandums of understanding.

Assembling a 737

Located about 20 miles south of Seattle in Washington and adjacent to the Renton Municipal Airport, the Boeing Commercial Airplanes' Renton facility has been home to many of the company's most renowned aircraft, including the 707, 727 and 757, but it is the 737 for which the site is most famous.

The site encompasses 4.3 million square feet of building space and is where all 737s, including the P-8 and the Boeing Business Jets, are produced. The facility had two production lines for 737NGs, and a new production line was built for the 737 MAX. The site includes manufacturing employees building the 737s, engineers and technical employees supporting the in-production aircraft.

Two high-bay final assembly buildings encompass 1.1 million square feet and include offices for engineers, executives, and support staff. Boeing said in 2016 it had initiated 145 projects to upgrade the site infrastructure and improve the production systems at Renton since 2010 to position the site for 737 MAX production. The 737 MAX build process was designed to maintain maximum compatibility with 737NG assembly.

Fuselages are produced by Spirit AeroSystems in Wichita, Kansas and transported by train on a 2,175-mile ride across the United States. After arrival at Renton the first stage is to install insulation material along the inside walls of the fuselage, then add wiring and ducting.

Near the beginning of the moving line, an overhead crane lifts the 23ft-high tailfin into place so it can be attached. The crane then lifts the fuselage and places it down into position, where precision tools are used to install the fin as well as the landing gear and wings.

Wing assembly itself takes place in a separate building at Renton using a horizontal assembly process where special tools raise and lower the wings to an ergonomically correct height for mechanics to work on the top or bottom, and hand tools are counter-weighted to reduce strain on the workers. Wing production uses a moving line to assemble wing panels that includes machines to do repetitive work such as installing fasteners.

Originally 737s were assembled in one spot but they are now produced on a moving assembly line. Henry Ford introduced the moving line to automobile manufacturing a century ago to help reduce assembly time and cut inventory and production costs; Boeing first used the concept on the 717.

The 737s on the line move continuously at a rate of two inches per minute; the line stops only for employee breaks, critical production issues or between shifts. Timelines painted on the floor help workers gauge the progress of manufacturing. Near the beginning of the moving line, an overhead crane lifts the 23ft-high tailfin into place so it can be attached. Next, floor panels and serving galleys are installed and functional testing begins.

The aircraft is pressurised in a test called the 'high blow' to ensure there are no air leaks and the structure is sound. In another test, the aircraft is jacked up so that the landing gear retraction and extension systems can be tested. As the aircraft moves closer to the end of the line, the cabin interior is completed – seats, lavatories, luggage bins, ceiling panels, carpets, etc. The final stage is to mount the engines.

After rollout and painting, aircraft are towed across the Cedar River to the pre-flight area at the adjacent Renton Municipal Airport, west of the main site. Following the initial test flight, the aircraft land at Boeing Field in Seattle where final preparations are made for delivery to customers.

THIS IMAGE • *The 737's production line moves at two inches per minute.* BOEING

LEFT • *Spars for a 737 MAX wing being loaded into an automated spar assembly machine.* BOEING

The largest single order was for 100 examples from United Airlines. Other major commitments came from the Lion Air Group (50) and SpiceJet (40), with a clutch of carriers (mainly from the Asia-Pacific region) and leasing companies making up the remainder of customers.

Andrew Levy, United Airlines' executive vice-president and chief financial officer at the time, said of United's 100-aircraft order: "The 737 MAX 10 will enable us to continue using larger and more efficient aircraft within our domestic network."

Levy's comment goes to the heart of the business case underpinning the 737 MAX 10: capacity. A big trend among operators in the single-aisle airliner market in the 2010s was ordering aircraft with more seats.

This so-called 'up-gauging' stems from industry economics: more seats maximise load factors, reduce seat-mile costs and increase revenues. The 737 MAX 10's launch was partly to take advantage of this trend.

It was also an attempt by Boeing to regain lost ground at the top end of the seating scale in the narrowbody aircraft market. The Airbus A321, the largest A320 Family variant, which seats 185 passengers two-class or 236 single-class, sold well in both its A321ceo and A321neo guises, with 1,700 A321ceos and 1,400 A321neos sold by Airbus at the time of the 737 MAX 10's 2017 launch.

The 737 MAX 10 is designed to compete directly with the A321 and on its launch Boeing claimed the 737 MAX 10 would offer 5% lower trip costs and 5% lower seat-mile costs than its competitor.

BBJ MAX Variants

By the time of the 737 MAX 10's launch Boeing had also offered business jet versions of their latest 737 models, launching the BBJ MAX 7, BBJ MAX 8, and BBJ MAX 9 on April 2, 2014.

On launching these aircraft, the company said the new models would provide more room and longer range than the earlier BBJs while providing the same lower fuel burn and performance advantages. The improvements were brought by the 737 MAX's more fuel-efficient CFM International LEAP-1B ✈

The 737 MAX's CFM International LEAP-1B turbofans, the engines replacing the 737NG's CFM56-7Bs, are one of the principal changes between the two generations, boasting a 69.4in fan diameter compared to the 61in fan diameter on the CFM56-7Bs.

engines, improved aerodynamics (including the AT Winglets) and advanced systems.

As with the earlier BBJ versions of the 737 developed in the 1990s, the BBJ MAX versions are offered with a range of supplemental fuel tanks in both the forward and aft cargo holds to extend range, with customers selecting their preferred tank arrangement based on their operational requirements.

Boeing's Airplane Characteristics for Airport Planning document does not list auxiliary fuel capacity for the BBJ MAX 7, the smallest variant, but capacity on the BBJ MAX 8 is up to 10,394 US gal in up to 11 tanks and up to 10,921 US gal in 13 tanks can be fitted into a BBJ MAX 9.

Boeing figures state the BBJ MAX 7 has 7,000nm range, over 730nm more than the BBJ. The BBJ MAX 8 can fly 6,640nm, which is 1,010nm further than a BBJ2, and the BBJ MAX 9's 6,515nm capability is 970nm more than the BBJ3.

The BBJ MAX 7 cabin is 85ft 8in long, 6ft 4in longer than the BBJ1 cabin, creating 884 sq ft total area. The BBJ MAX 8 cabin is 98ft 6in long with 1,025 sq ft area, longer than the BBJ2's, and the BBJ MAX 9 cabin is 107ft 6in long, offering 1,120 sq ft area, again larger than the BBJ3.

At the time of the BBJ MAX's launch, Boeing Business Jets' then-president, Steve Taylor, said: "We expect a large demand for the BBJ MAX, particularly from those BBJ owners who want to fly farther and more efficiently and still maintain the exceptional comfort of a BBJ."

In April 2018, four years after launch, the first completed BBJ MAX aircraft, a BBJ MAX 8, flew away from Boeing's Renton production site for completion after completing factory rollout, first flight and testing. At that moment nearly 20 BBJ MAX aircraft had been ordered spanning all three models.

A Boeing statement issued at the time said: "BBJ MAX owners benefit from a lower total cost to own when compared to other high-end business jets. The MAX's optimised maintenance schedule drives operating costs that are nearly the same as smaller, less comfortable competitors. BBJs also retain comparatively higher residual values by requiring a fraction of the lengthy and expensive shop visits experienced by other business jets as they age. As a result, the BBJ MAX can save customers millions of dollars in total ownership expenditure over the life of the airplane."

Lower Fuel Burn

When launching a refreshed version of an established product, aircraft manufacturers must introduce new technologies that will make a tangible difference to the aircraft's economics while retaining elements that made it popular in the first place.

The 737 MAX's CFM International LEAP-1B turbofans, the engines replacing the 737NG's CFM56-7Bs, are one of the principal changes between the two generations, boasting a 69.4in fan diameter compared to the 61in fan diameter on the CFM56-7Bs.

The larger fan size, and therefore larger engine nacelles, than the CFM56-7Bs meant Boeing had to extend the nose landing gear by 8in to ensure sufficient clearance between the LEAP-1Bs and the ground, resulting in the 737 MAX sitting slightly higher on the ground compared to the 737NG.

737 MAX 7 Characteristics

Length	116ft 8in
Height	40ft 4in
Wingspan	117ft 10in
Max take-off weight	177,000lb
Max landing weight	145,600lb
Max zero fuel weight	138,700lb
Useable fuel	6,820 US gal
Engines	2x CFM International LEAP-1Bs
Max cruise speed	Mach 0.79
Ceiling	41,000ft
Range	3,850nm
Seats	153 two-class, 172 single-class

737 MAX 8/737 MAX 200 Characteristics

Length	129ft 6in
Height	40ft 4in
Wingspan	117ft 10in
Max take-off weight	181,700lb
Max landing weight	152,800lb
Max zero fuel weight	145,400lb
Useable fuel	6,820 US gal
Engines	2x CFM International LEAP-1Bs
Max cruise speed	Mach 0.79
Ceiling	41,000ft
Range	3,550nm
Seats	178 two-class or 189 single-class (737 MAX 8), 200 (737 MAX 200)

Boeing said the 737 MAX will burn 14% less fuel than the 737NG, or 20% less compared to the first NGs produced in the 1990s. The LEAP-1Bs account for 11% of the reduction. Boeing claims that when compared to a fleet of 100 737 NGs the MAX will emit 310,000 tonnes less carbon dioxide and save 215 million pounds of fuel per year.

In addition to lower fuel burn and emissions, the 737 MAX also offered increased maximum take-off weight, maximum zero fuel weight and maximum landing weight, which led to increased material sizing to support higher weights and local changes to the landing gear doghouse and radar bay.

Design Features

A key change from the 737NG were all-new Advanced Technology (AT) Winglets, which combine upwards-facing and downwards-facing aerofoils, rather than just an upwards-facing aerofoil as on the Blended Winglet, to improve the wing's performance.

Other significant differences in the 737 MAX's design from the 737NG include an extended tail cone housing a redesigned auxiliary power unit inlet and a thicker tail cross-section above

the elevator to improve the steadiness of the airflow around the tail. Boeing says these changes will eliminate the need for vortex generators on the tail and reduce drag by 1%, contributing to the fuel burn improvement.

The spoilers are electronically controlled, and there is a Honeywell electronic bleed air system to provide wing anti-ice protection and cabin

pressurisation and environmental control. On the 737NG, the spoilers and bleed air system were all hydraulically controlled. Using electronic controls means the number of hydraulic components such as valves and ducting that were required for these systems has been reduced, which translates into a weight saving and a fuel efficiency gain.

The increased ground clearance

BOEING BUSINESS JETS

6843

to accommodate the larger engines was achieved by moving the nosewheel undercarriage bay bulkhead forwards. A blister fairing was added beneath the nose and local strengthening work undertaken on wing spars, skins, some fuselage structures, and the landing gear.

Boeing says the integration between the engines and the wing has also been improved to reduce drag and contribute to fuel efficiency. The LEAP-1B engines themselves also have an all-new nacelle and secondary chevrons on the thrust reverser to reduce noise.

Commonality

Despite the differences in the 737 MAX, Boeing sought to maximise commonality with the 737NG.

Structural architecture remains common with the previous generation, which enabled Boeing to use the existing production system, supply chain and support arrangements to help 737NG operators that have ordered the 737 MAX in big numbers such as Southwest Airlines and Ryanair, integrate the new 737 into their fleets efficiently.

According to Boeing's chief test pilot at the time, Captain Ed Wilson, despite the 737 MAX having four large MFDs, just one panel – which houses the switches that control the autobrakes – was moved in the cockpit, to the lower aisle stand in front of the thrust levers. Everything else, including the overhead panel, is in the same position as on the 737NG.

Another aspect of commonality between the NG and MAX flight decks is provision for Boeing's integrated approach navigation functionality, designed to provide instrument landing system-like procedures, display features

and autopilot control laws for non-precision approaches. It is an option on the 737NG and remains so on the MAX for customers who want it.

Boeing's Sky Interior cabin with sculpted sidewalls, larger windows, and bigger overhead stowage bins, introduced on the 737NG in 2011, is the standard cabin design on the 737 MAX.

There are however some differences between the Sky Interior on the two generations. The 737 MAX's electronic bleed air system provides a constant flow of air to the cabin, unlike the 737NG, and the 737 MAX's version features larger overhead stowage bins called Space Bins that carry six standard-sized bags, two more than the

ABOVE • *A BBJ MAX 9 during a test flight.* BOEING

BELOW • *Qatar Airways is among those to have ordered the 737 MAX 10.* BOEING

bins in the Sky Interior on the 737NG.

Boeing said: "Airlines can expect quicker boarding and turnaround processes at the gate. With a lower bin lip height, Space Bins provide increased visibility into the back of the bins and make bag loading even easier. They're also as easy to close as the current pivot bins yet require no bin assist mechanism to facilitate closure."

737 MAX 9 Characteristics

Length	138ft 2in
Height	40ft 4in
Wingspan	117ft 10in
Max take-off weight	194,700lb
Max landing weight	163,900lb
Max zero fuel weight	156,500lb
Useable fuel	6,820 US gal
Engines	2x CFM International LEAP-1Bs
Max cruise speed	Mach 0.79
Ceiling	41,000ft
Range	3,550nm
Seats	193 two-class, 220 single-class

737 MAX 10 Characteristics

Length	143ft 8in
Height	40ft 4in
Wingspan	117ft 10in
Max take-off weight	197,900lb
Max landing weight	167,400lb
Max zero fuel weight	160,000lb
Useable fuel	6,820 US gal
Engines	2x CFM International LEAP-1Bs
Max cruise speed	Mach 0.79
Ceiling	41,000ft
Range	3,330nm
Seats	204 two-class, 230 single-class

Milestones

Firm configuration of the 737 MAX 8's design was achieved in July 2013. Boeing began assembling the wing for the first flight test aircraft at Renton, the home of the 737, in May 2015. The initial fuselage arrived at the factory that August after being transported by rail from subcontractor Spirit AeroSystems in Wichita, Kansas.

Following systems integration and the joining of the wings to the fuselage, the landing gear, tail, flight systems and LEAP-1Bs were installed. The aircraft, N8701Q (c/n 42554) Spirit of Renton – also known simply as Airplane 1 – was rolled-out on December 8, 2015. After engine and taxi tests, it flew on January 29, 2016.

A further three flight test aircraft, N8702L (c/n 36989, or Airplane 2), N8703J (c/n 42556, Airplane 3) and N8704Q (c/n 36988, Airplane 4), joined the flight testing and certification programme during 2016.

Airplane 2 flew on March 4, Airplane 3 on April 14, and Airplane 4 on May 7. Airplane 1 was used for stability and control tests, Airplane 2 for performance, Airplane 3 for propulsion and systems and Airplane 4 for function and reliability (F&R).

The flight-test programme was run from Boeing Field at Seattle, but other locations were used for certain tests. El Alto International Airport in La Paz, Bolivia hosted Airplane 2 for high-altitude testing. The same aircraft went to Glasgow in Montana for water spray testing and community noise assessments and to Yuma, Arizona for high temperature evaluations. Airplane 3 went to Edwards AFB, California, and Colorado Springs for autoland systems tests.

The 737 MAX 8 received US Federal Aviation Administration certification on March 8, 2017. Launch operator Batik Air in Malaysia started revenue operations with its first example, 9M-LRC (c/n 42985) in May 2017 on return flights on the relatively short (45-50 minutes) Singapore to Kuala Lumpur route.

On April 13, 2017, the initial 737 MAX 9, N7379E (c/n 42987) undertook its maiden flight from Renton (landing back at Boeing Field) and entered testing. This aircraft, also known as 1D001, was used for flutter, stability/control, autoland and avionics testing. A second jet, N739EX (c/n 42989, aka 1D002) was used for environmental control testing.

The 737 MAX 9 received FAA certification in February 2018 before Lion Air put its first example into service on March 21, 2018, with an EASA type certificate following in October 2018.

The 737 MAX 7 flew from Renton on March 16, 2018 and landed at Moses Lake, Washington after a three-hour flight. At the time of the aircraft's initial flight, Boeing targeted an early 2019 service entry for the variant but launch operator Southwest Airlines deferred its orders to 2023/2024 and WestJet converted its order into 737 MAX 8s.

Boeing rolled out the initial 737 MAX 10 at Renton on November 22, 2019. At the time the company said the largest 737 MAX would fly during 2020 after undergoing system checks and engine runs. At the time of writing in November 2020, this largest 737 MAX variant was yet to conduct that initial flight.

Boeing does not break down information on 737 MAX orders by variant, but at the time of writing there were 5,263 total orders for the family according to the company's latest updated orders and deliveries data.

Systems
Evolution

Mark Broadbent profiles some of the key
systems developments on the 737.

*An Onboard Network
System is a new feature
on the 737 MAX.* BOEING/
MARIAN LOCKHART

The 737's systems architecture largely follows the established and conventional form for an airliner, with engine bleed air driving generators that power aircraft pressurisation, engine and auxiliary power unit (APU) start, engine and wing anti-ice protection, hydraulics, electrics and the cabin environmental control system.

However, on a product family that has been around for half a century there have inevitably been developments in systems functionality with each generation of the aircraft. On the 737-100/737-200 there was full hydromechanical control of aircraft systems. Electronic supervisory control, which is traditional hydromechanical control with electronic trim, was introduced on the 737 Classics.

The 737 Next Generation (737NG) brought a significant step forward, with the aircraft's propulsion control system (PCS) using electronically based full-authority digital electronic engine control (FADEC). The latest 737 MAX has introduced further modernisation including increased connectivity.

Electronic Control

According to Boeing, the differences to the PCS on the 737NG compared to the traditional architecture on earlier 737s fell into three categories: components and installations, flight operations, and maintenance.

On the 737 original and Classic versions PCS functions such as engine fuel on/off control and thrust set were completed mechanically by control cables, but on the 737NG these controls and the interfaces between them and key aircraft systems were digitalised.

Electronic engine control (EEC), installed on the fan case of each engine,

is the primary PCS component. The EEC receives inputs from the aircraft and engine sensors, computes the desired engine thrust and sends electrical commands to the various actuators to make the engine accelerate or decelerate to the desired thrust.

An EEC alternator installed on the forward face of the accessory gearbox supplies primary electrical power for the aircraft's systems. The EEC additionally acquires, processes, and outputs data for the flight deck displays and for maintenance. It also detects and accommodates faults. A hydromechanical unit, installed on the aft-left side of the accessory gearbox on the engine, controls fuel flow to the engine and other valves.

The EEC and its impact on functionality compared with earlier 737s was designed to be invisible to flight crews, enabling 737 Classic and 737NG flight crews to retain the same type rating.

As a technical outline published by Boeing in its AERO in-house publication in 1998 stressed: "Though the FADEC-based PCS contains several enhancements, the flight crew will notice few changes from earlier 737s."

For example, the crew use the same levers and switches for engine control, although the commands for engine thrust and deploying thrust reversers sent along the connecting rods beneath the floor are now sent by electrical signals rather than mechanical cables.

Operations

The PCS equipment interfaces with other key systems aboard such as common display system, the flight management system, and the autothrottle, and ARINC-429 digital databases transfer data between the EECs and these systems for ✈

Various connectivity systems are available to link the 737 MAX Onboard Network System with the crew aboard and an operator's ground infrastructure.

efficient integrated operation.

Several new features were introduced such as automatic protection to help prevent engine damage in the event of an abnormal ground engine start. These include a feature stopping fuel and ignition if the exhaust gas temperature does not increase within 15 seconds after the engine start lever is moved to idle. There is hot start protection (which stops fuel and ignition if the engine temperature exceeds the start limit of 725oC), rollback protection (which stops ignition if the engine, once started, decelerates to less than a sustainable idle speed), and flameout protection.

Other new PCS innovations were a no-dispatch alert through the illumination of an amber ENGINE CONTROL light on the aft overhead control panel in the cockpit notifying the crew of an engine control fault, new power management control switches, and an alternate thrust-setting mode. Engine indications were enhanced with the additions of new indicators for the reverser, engine acceleration and deceleration, thermal anti-ice status, temperature, and oil pressure.

Maintenance

The 737NG's PCS meant maintenance procedures differed in some respects from earlier 737s.

One crucial difference is the EEC system logic enables an engine to operate normally when faults exist. For example, a complete failure of one EEC channel has no immediate effect on engine operation because a second channel takes over.

The ENGINE CONTROL lights and messages on the flight management computer and common display unit maintenance screens report non-obvious faults. As time-limited-dispatch faults are not indicated to the flight crew, maintenance personnel must periodically use the flight management computer/control display unit (FMC/CDU) maintenance pages to check for them.

The CDU menu pages enable maintenance personnel to check for faults in each dispatch category; perform functional tests; check for engine speed or temperature exceedances; monitor EEC input signals; and review the engine control configuration.

The propulsion controls have several built-in tests that are accessed through the FMC/CDU maintenance pages for key systems such as the autothrottle, designed to help maintainers identify and solve problems quickly.

OPPOSITE • *The 737NG brought considerable advances to the aircraft's propulsion control system.* AIRTEAMIMAGES/ ANDRES MENESES

BELOW • *Electronic engine control, installed on the fan case of each engine, is the primary PCS component on the 737NG.* AIRTEAMIMAGES/RUDI BOIGELOT

More than 75 flight hours of operational data for onboard and offboard analytics can be collected thanks to a mass storage functionality hosted by the Onboard Network System file server called ONS Quick Access Recorder.

Onboard Network System

The 737 MAX was designed to retain the 737NG's systems functionality and procedures to help ensure commonality for flight and maintenance crews, but there is one crucial systems difference on the latest-generation aircraft: an Onboard Network System (ONS).

In a 2014 edition of its AERO publication explaining the ONS, Boeing said the new system is: "designed to enhance and extend the Next-Generation 737 while maintaining commonality with the previous models."

Described by Boeing as "a network of on-airplane systems" that integrates the aircraft's data-rich systems with optional connectivity systems, the ONS is intended "to make the 737 MAX a node on the airline's network" by securely connecting an operator's flight operations and maintenance teams with key aircraft data and software.

By increasing the quantity of available data about the aircraft and making it readily available to the crew and the airline's ground infrastructure, the ONS is intended to seamlessly support an operator by increasing all maintenance tasks, engineering, procedures, and ground operations support.

Boeing said: "For example, an airline maintenance team may leverage data collected across the 737 MAX fleet for predictive maintenance analytics. An ONS-connected airplane will be able to take advantage of services from Boeing that can further optimize airplane operations."

Hardware and Connectivity

Several pieces of key hardware are part of the 737 MAX onboard network.

The hub of the ONS is a file server housed in the electronics equipment bay. This connects to a large set of data-rich systems, houses hundreds of gigabytes of mass data storage, sends maintenance data to flight deck displays, and hosts onboard and offboard data processing functions. Direct connection between the file server and the airline's maintenance device is provided by a flight deck Ethernet port or optional connectivity systems.

Another piece of ONS hardware is an enhanced digital flight data acquisition unit (DFDAU). Following an October 1991 US Federal Aviation Administration rule change, Boeing introduced DFDAUs on all its airliners to increase the amount of flight information collected in an aircraft's flight data recorders. For the 737 MAX the DFDAU was upgraded to make 100 times more data available than the equipment on earlier-generation 737s.

Finally, the 737 MAX's display system is connected to the ONS file server to further increase data availability and to enable flight deck display of maintenance information on the large-format displays.

Various connectivity systems are available to link the 737 MAX ONS with the crew aboard and an operator's ground infrastructure.

There's a secure Wi-Fi network aboard the aircraft for crew and ground/maintenance use, both in-flight and at the gate. This system can integrate with crew mobile devices for paperless operational and maintenance procedures.

Additionally, a broadband internet

protocol (IP) connectivity system makes the 737 MAX capable of wireless transfer of data or software parts between the ONS file server and the airline's ground-based offices using the secure Wi-Fi or cellular connections while the airplane is on the ground.

The ONS can also be integrated with IP-based satellite connectivity systems on the L-band, Ku, and Ka wavelengths to facilitate secure high-speed data transfer in flight.

Consolidation

The ONS is designed to consolidate existing functions typically performed by several optional systems by integrating data loading, recording and system troubleshooting into a single system, including functions typically performed by a crew's electronic flight bags (EFBs). The ONS may also be combined with Boeing's other data and analytics services for advanced maintenance planning.

Additionally, there is also commonality with the 737NG's systems architecture. Boeing noted: "The system available on the Next-Generation 737 is equipped with connections to the same or equivalent Onboard Network System Provisions."

Overall, Boeing says: "Particularly when paired with connectivity, ONS consolidates a powerful set of capabilities including data load, airplane data recording, system fault reporting, and health management onto a single integrated system."

New Functionality

The ONS file server is connected to all data-loadable systems on the 737 MAX, which gives several new areas of functionality on the 737NG.

Boeing explains: "ONS is unique in its capability to load software parts over highspeed Ethernet, greatly decreasing the time required to load Ethernet-enabled systems such as the display system."

More than 75 flight hours of operational data for onboard and offboard analytics can be collected thanks to a mass storage functionality hosted by the ONS file server called ONS Quick Access Recorder (QAR). This system houses secure data and software distribution and, when paired with a connectivity system and ground-based system integration software, makes possible secure wireless

electronic distribution of software and data between the aircraft and airline.

Crew applications running on portable maintenance devices, such as tablets, may connect to the ONS file server for services such as onboard storage, printing, airplane data, and offboard connectivity.

Exclusive Functionality

Certain aspects of the ONS are available only on the 737 MAX.

The 737 MAX display system integrates data collected during flight with a new onboard maintenance function that consolidates maintenance data for viewing on the large flight deck displays or on portable maintenance devices such as tablets.

Data displayed in the flight deck includes system dispatch status, existing faults, initiated tests, configuration

ABOVE • The ONS on the 737 MAX is designed to be combined with Boeing's data and analytics services for advanced maintenance planning.
BOEING

reporting, and maintenance page information. According to Boeing, this onboard maintenance function is "capable of reducing no-fault found events by correlating system status indications to detailed system and equipment faults and...allow for fault forwarding downlinks."

Boeing explains: "Centralising the display of this information allows the creation of common maintenance procedures and allows mechanics to perform maintenance and fault isolation tasks for each of the 737 MAX systems without accessing them individually in the electronics equipment bay."

This is designed to provide more focused maintenance troubleshooting.

A further change on the 737 MAX is that the functions of the airborne vibration monitor and EEC are integrated into a single line replaceable unit. Boeing says the integration of the EEC into the ONS offers advanced engine health management including enhanced trim balance and prognostics

reports, and increased engine data collection for in-service maintenance support and performance analysis.

Overall, the company says: "The quantity of data made available by the 737 MAX ONS facilitates advances in all aspects of operations, including maintenance, engineering, and ground operations. An ONS-connected airplane will be able to take advantage of services from Boeing that can further optimise airplane operations."

More Evolution

Boeing added: "As connected airspace evolves; the 737 MAX will be equipped with security measures to protect airplane and passenger information that is transferred on and off the airplane. The 737 MAX ONS will meet FAA data security guidance to create a safe and secure airborne network.

"The new ONS is a secure, scalable, and integrated architecture that enables significant operational and maintenance efficiencies by connecting critical airplane data with the airline and its ground infrastructure."

The Next Generation 737 flight deck. BOEING

Flight Deck

Mark Broadbent outlines the evolution of the 737's flight deck over the years.

The appearance and functionality of the 737's flight deck has moved in step with advances in flight deck technology through the decades.

Classic 'round dial' mechanical instrumentation was used in the 737-100 and the early 737-200 for the key flight instruments such as the attitude indicator, attitude direction indicator, artificial horizon, horizontal situation indicator, airspeed indicator, vertical speed indicator (VSI) and engine instruments. There was no flight management computer (FMC).

The 737-200 Advanced used an early version of the ARINC 500 series which included an automated flight director system, two FMC cockpit display units (CDUs) with digital colour weather radar, digital total air temperature, dual electric Mach/airspeed, altimeter and a VSI with dual digital ADCs were added.

737 Classics

On the 737 Classic models, the primary flight instruments remained arranged in the basic 'T' scan layout. Early 737-300s continued to be largely analogue using the ARINC 500 series flight instrumentation. Engine instruments on the 737 Classic remained largely electromechanical, with data displayed in rolling digits and multiple green LED segments serving as pointers.

Certain flight deck functions also continued to require manual input. Crews had to manipulate sliding white plastic 'bugs' around the ring of the Mach airspeed indicator (MASI) to indicate take-off and landing speeds and move switches on the radio distance magnetic indicators to select the automatic direction finder or very-high-frequency omni range.

Boeing did adopt some automation for later 737-300s and the other 737 Classic models by adopting an optional electronic flight instrumentation system (EFIS) with cathode ray tube (CRT) displays. This provided more concise flight information and reduced the crew's workload by showing the

The 737 MAX 7 variant has what Boeing calls a high-altitude package optimised for hot and high environments. This features engines with higher thrust, an alternate forward centre of gravity for improved take-off weight, an auxiliary battery for 60-minute standby power, a gaseous oxygen system with up to 12 cylinders, and advanced avionics.

primary electronic attitude direction indicator (EADI) and the electronic horizontal situation indicator (EHSI).

The EADI presentation includes autothrottle, mode annunciation, autopilot mode annunciation, and vertical speed tape options. Weather radar and traffic collision avoidance system (TCAS) data are superimposed over the navigation data on the EHSI.

A further significant piece of automation introduced on the 737 Classic was the Speed Trim System (STS), a flight augmentation system designed to provide trim inputs to the horizontal stabiliser in manual flight, with flaps up, by automatically moving the stabiliser in response to changes from trimmed airspeed while in manual flight to provide speed stability.

737 Next Generation

Digital avionics technology moved forward enormously and when the 737NG was developed in the 1990s, Boeing was able to introduce an EFIS as standard to the 737's flight deck.

Key to the 737NG was the computer-generated graphic representation of flight instruments on the common display system (CDS), presented on six 8 x 8in LCD screens. This was designed to reproduce either one of two different instrument panels: the EFIS with map

panel on the 737 Classic (EFIS/MAP) or the primary flight display/navigational display (PFD/ND) panel from the 777 and 747-400. The CDS in the EFIS/MAP format was essentially the same as the EFIS/MAP flight deck in the 737-300, meaning flight crews using the CDS and its associated EFIS control panel had the same workload as they would on the 737-300.

According to a 1998 Boeing AERO article: "The task included incorporating new, improved digital technologies and the necessary attendant equipment while meeting the requirement to save airplane weight, reduce part numbers, and cut costs. This all had to be accomplished without losing the same type rating for flight crews who would use the new flight deck.

"The flight deck redesign initially appeared to require several visible changes to incorporate new digital systems, including at least 22 new parts and a complicated flight deck instrument panel made up of electromechanical and digital displays.

"However, a brand-new flight deck was not an option. Operators had clearly stated that they wanted no change to the type rating, no requirement for additional flight crew simulator training, and no new 'bells and whistles' without clear economic or safety value."

Instruments and Functionality

To retain commonality with the 737 Classic flight deck, Boeing minimised changes to the presentation of EFIS data and instruments, with the format of the CDS graphically generating the same 'round dial' format and presenting it in the 'T' scan pattern.

However, with the 737NG using full-authority digital-electronic engine control (FADEC) the analogue-based electromechanical instruments and flight crew interfaces of the 737 Classics were replaced by digital ARINC 700 series avionics.

A modern flight management system introduced weather radar, traffic collision avoidance system and an enhanced ground proximity warning system, with crews able to individually adjust the brightness of each display unit in response to sunlight.

The four display units located outboard and inboard on the captain's forward panel and first officer's forward panel show all primary flight and navigation data. The upper and lower-centre display units on the centre panel show engine and system data.

The CDS provides for automatic switching to handle failures of the display units, and internal monitoring of display unit failures. It automatically

BELOW • *The 737 MAX flight deck.* AIRTEAMIMAGES/ DIPANKAR BHAKTA

and there's no upper range defined."

Capt Wilson added: "It's a more enjoyable experience to fly with larger displays. The younger pilots that come along are more used to having larger displays in front of them. I think it's important that we continue to upgrade the aircraft to more what our pilots will like and use in the future."

The 737 MAX 7 variant has what Boeing calls a high-altitude package optimised for hot and high environments. This features engines with higher thrust, an alternate forward centre of gravity for improved take-off weight, an auxiliary battery for 60-minute standby power, a gaseous oxygen system with up to 12 cylinders, and advanced avionics for Required Navigation Performance Authorisation Required.

For the 737 MAX, Boeing introduced an additional pitch augmentation control

*ABOVE • **A 737 Classic flight deck.** BOEING*

*RIGHT • **The 737-200 flight deck.** BOEING*

maintains a primary flight display in view for all single failures, with crews having the option to manually place formats and select its source by using the display source selection.

A display source select switch and an EFIS control select switch located in the overhead panel enable a crew member to control both sides of the displays, with identical EFIS control functions shown at both crew member positions. Pilots can manually force the PFD to either the inboard or outboard display unit by using the display select panel, which also allows the crew member to manually move engine and other display formats to new locations.

The 737NG's CDS also enhanced the 737 flight deck by introducing colour and alphanumeric characters for certain indications or warnings. Examples include amber warnings on the fuel indicator (for FUEL CONFIGURATION, FUEL IMBALANCE, and LOW FUEL) and green or amber indication on the engine display for thermal anti-ice, ENGINE FAIL, and REV (reverser position).

737 MAX

The 737 MAX brought another advancement in the 737's flight deck. It has four 15.1in Rockwell Collins LCDs rather than the six smaller displays on the 737NG's flight deck.

Speaking in 2016, Captain Ed Wilson, then Boeing's chief pilot for the 737, told this author the larger MFDs made

a difference: "The primary flight display becomes a larger format display, so you can see it easier [and] make a better judgement about the aircraft attitude; and because we can use an entire screen now, the navigation display just becomes easier to interpret."

Capt Wilson said: "Where we follow what we call our magenta line, where we programme our flight, we can see across the navigation display. The navigation display on the NG only goes down to five miles range. Now we can go down to half-mile range to see more precisely,

law for the STS, the Manoeuvring Characteristics Augmentation System (MCAS). This control law affects pitch characteristics in manual flight, with flaps up and at elevated angles of attack, to compensate for the aerodynamic pitch effects associated with the 737 MAX's larger, more forward engines.

The MCAS was a factor in the Lion Air Flight 610 and Ethiopian Airlines Flight 302 crashes that led to the 737 MAX's grounding in March 2019. Boeing has now updated MCAS (see Return to Service).

Winglets

Mark Broadbent explains one
of the key developments on the 737.

From a distance the AT
Winglet resembles the
Split Scimitar, but closer
comparison shows it has
a raked design to redirect
vortices. BOEING

When Boeing was developing the Boeing Business Jet (BBJ) variants of the 737NG, the company obviously wanted to extract the best performance from the airframe so the BBJ could compete with the Bombardier Global Express and Gulfstream GV, the latest high-performance business jets of the time.

This led to the development of the Blended Winglets, the distinctive upwards-facing aerofoils on the wings designed to optimise performance and help increase range.

Understanding Loads

A 2002 article published in the Boeing *AERO* technical magazine explained the winglets' development.

The aft component of air deflected by a wing is known as induced drag, and its exact magnitude depends on the profile of a wing's trailing edge.

Induced drag can be minimised by increasing the trailing edge length but extending span increases weight. NASA research found a solution to this quandary: a winglet could redirect vortices, enabling the performance benefit to be achieved while minimising additional weight.

Accommodating winglets has an impact. For example, the highest loads on the mid to outboard part of a wing occur when speed brakes are extended, with the inboard portion of the wing reaching its highest loads in the clean wing configuration. The outboard section of a wing generally is designed for roll manoeuvres, but winglets cause a higher loading on the outboard area.

Gusts or turbulence further affect airframe behaviour, while the weight of a winglet itself, its extreme outboard location, and the associated structural changes to accommodate the devices, all affect static loads, dynamic flight loads, the centre of gravity and flutter characteristics.

Tests and Development

To develop a satisfactory product that accounted for all these factors while meeting performance requirements, Boeing gathered technical data on aerodynamics, loads and flutter.

Wind tunnel tests of an initial winglet design determined the change in air load distribution on the wing caused by winglets. This was used to minimise the adverse effects of the higher loads caused by adding the winglets.

Flight tests provided further data on loads, handling qualities, and aerodynamic performance. Strain gauges and rows of pressure taps placed on the prototype winglet and outboard wing recorded changes in bending on the outboard wing.

The resulting data was used to adjust and validate the aerodynamic database created by the wind tunnel tests. All the tests determined a gross fuel burn improvement was recorded in the range of 4-5%. Accounting for the weight of the winglet and the related wing structural modifications, the net performance improvement was approximately 4% for long-range flights.

Using the test results, a refined winglet configuration was developed that combined the benefits of aerodynamic performance against the weight and cost of modifying the aircraft.

This 'blended' configuration was designed and patented in 1997 by Dr LB Gratzer of a Seattle-based company, Aviation Partners, Inc, which formed a joint venture with Boeing called Aviation Partners Boeing (APB).

The AERO technical article explained: "The aerodynamic advantage of a Blended Winglet is in the transition from the existing wingtip to the vertical winglet. The Blended Winglet allows for the chord distribution to change smoothly from the wingtip to the winglet, which optimises the distribution of the span load lift and minimises any aerodynamic interference or airflow separation."

It added: "The optimal configuration reduced loads and minimised weight and structural modifications without sacrificing significant winglet performance. It was achieved by an iterative process during which trade-offs among critical design functions were continually reviewed by experts in aerodynamics, loads, flutter, design, and stress."

Into Service

Blended Winglets entered service when the first BBJ was delivered to

APB's Split Scimitar uses the installed Blended Winglets' structure, with the aluminium cap replaced by a sharply swept-back tip (hence the scimitar name). A ventral strake, also featuring a scimitar tip, is attached to the lower part of the winglet.

its customer on September 4, 1999. The device was then certified for the 737-800 on March 23, 2001, with Hapag-Lloyd Airlines (today part of TUI) the first carrier to introduce a winglet-equipped 737-800 two months later.

The devices proved hugely popular. In 2003 APB reported 280 737NGs had received them in the two years since their service entry. By 2020, more than 5,000 were fitted to 737NGs.

APB developed a retrofit version of the winglets for the 737 Classics called the SP (Special Performance). The first kits, for 737-300s, were delivered in May 2003. At 7ft long the SP is slightly shorter than the 8ft 2in-long Blended Winglet, but according to APB still provide a 4.5% drag reduction on the Classic to a standard non-winglet equipped jet, saving operators 65,000 US gal of fuel per year.

Split Scimitar Winglet

In 2013 APB launched the Split Scimitar Winglet as a retrofit for all 737NGs to replace the Blended Winglets, later making it available as a standard production line-fit.

The Split Scimitar uses the installed Blended Winglets' structure, with the aluminium cap replaced by a sharply swept-back tip (hence the scimitar name). A ventral strake, also featuring a scimitar tip, is attached to the lower part of the winglet.

APB says the Split Scimitars provide an additional 1.5% reduction in block fuel consumption over Blended Winglets. The extra saving prompted a rush from 737NG operators to order Split Scimitars, with APB receiving orders for 1,451 examples within a few months of its launch.

United Airlines was the first carrier to have its 737NGs outfitted with the devices, with other early customers including Southwest Airlines, Alaska Airlines and TUI.

In September 2019, APB said the device had reduced fuel consumption worldwide by over ten billion gallons and saved over 105 million tons of carbon dioxide emissions. By that point

> *Accommodating winglets has an impact. For example, the highest loads on the mid to outboard part of a wing occur when speed brakes are extended, with the inboard portion of the wing reaching its highest loads in the clean wing configuration. The outboard section of a wing generally is designed for roll manoeuvres, but winglets cause a higher loading on the outboard area.*

BELOW • *The Boeing Business Jet precipitated the winglet's development.* BOEING

orders and options had been received for 2,300 Split Scimitars and installed on 1,200 aircraft.

AT Winglet

The 737 MAX features the Advanced Technology (AT) Winglet, specifically designed for the aircraft, with distinctive upwards-facing and downwards-facing aerofoils.

The upwards-facing aerofoil is designed to vector the inward, upward, and slightly forward lift components of the airflow around the wing to reduce lift-induced drag and improve laminar flow - if airflow over a wing is laminar, or smooth, there is less drag.

As noted above, the presence of a winglet itself creates induced drag. The AT Winglet's lower aerofoil is designed to generate a further vertical lift component that is then vectored away from the fuselage and slightly forwards.

The combination of this vertical lift component generated by the lower aerofoil and the benefits of the upper aerofoil result in what Boeing claims on its website to be "the perfectly balanced winglet that maximises the overall efficiency of the wing."

These differ from the 737NG's Blended Winglets by combining upwards-facing and downwards-facing aerofoils, rather than just an upwards-facing aerofoil as on the Blended Winglet, to improve the wing's performance.

The 737 MAX design team incorporated what Boeing calls advanced natural laminar flow technology – some of which was researched using the Boeing ecoDemonstrator Programme – into the surface material specification for the AT Winglet.

Boeing said: "The overall combination of advanced design and advanced airflow control means that the AT Winglet delivers the greatest contribution to improved fuel efficiency of any winglet."

Boeing says the AT Winglets contribute 1.8% of the 737 MAX's overall 14% fuel efficiency improvement from the 737NG.

Boeing 737
Conversions

Many Boeing 737s have found secondary uses as freighters. **Mark Broadbent** profiles the different options available.

ozen of 737s, both Classic-era versions (737-300s, 737-400s and 737-500s) and increasingly Next Generation examples (737-600s, 737-700s, 737-800s and 737-900s), fly as converted freighters.

Aeronautical Engineers Inc

Miami, Florida-based Aeronautical Engineers Inc (AEI) holds supplementary type certificates (STCs) for an 11-pallet 737-400 conversion, ten-pallet, and nine-pallet 737-300 conversions, eight pallets for the 737-200, and 11 pallets for the 737-800. All AEI-converted aircraft are re-designated as 737SFs.

Modification work involves installing a cargo door on the left fuselage and modifying the main deck to a Class E cargo compartment. The cargo door is hydraulically operated and actuated. Hydraulic pressure for this system is available from a 28VDC electrically operated hydraulic pump or a manual hand pump.

Other changes are the introduction of a single vent door system, the replacement of cabin windows with lightweight aluminium window plugs, and the installation of a 9g rigid cargo/smoke barrier with a sliding door. There are four additional seats for non-flying crew.

On the 737-400SF and 737-300SF, the cargo door measures 86 x 140in. The 737-400SF's main deck has capacity for ten 88 x 125in unit load device (ULD) containers or pallets and 47,100lb payload.

The 737-300SF is the only 737-300 freighter conversion with nine or ten positions. It accommodates up to eight ULDs and two half containers up to 42,900lb. The 737-200SF conversion features an 86 x 137in door and offers 37,800lb payload comprising seven 88 x 125 containers and one 88 x 108 pallet.

As with the conversions for the older jets, the 737-800SF STC installs an 86in x 140in door and modifies the main deck to a Class E cargo compartment. However, the 737-800's greater length increases capacity: a 737-800SF can carry 11 88 x 125in full height containers or pallets plus one AEP/AEH up to a 52,000lb payload. Additionally, the 737-800SF includes five supernumerary seats, a galley and lavatory.

AEI Orders

AEI has developed over 128 STCs and modified more than 500 aircraft since it was founded in 1958. As well as Boeings, it currently offers conversions for MD-80 series and CRJ200 aircraft.

The relentless growth of e-commerce has prompted increased demand for small package deliveries, which has stimulated demand for 737-sized freighters.

Since the start of 2020, AEI has announced 26 orders for its 737 conversions from customers including Aero Capital Solutions (four examples), Allied Air (up to four examples), Aviation Holdings Investments III, LLC (three aircraft) and GA Telesis (two). The conversions for both 737 Classics and some 737NGs.

The company offers a nine-pallet configuration for the 737-300 (eight full-size container or pallets and one smaller container or pallet) with a 43,100lb (19,500kg) maximum payload. It also has a quick-change option for the 737-300 that enables a 147-seat all-economy layout to be changed to a cargo layout of eight full-size containers within 30 minutes.

For the 737-400 PEMCO offers an 11-position 'high yield freighter' with 4,600 cu ft main deck volume, a 48,000lb payload for handling the various sizes of industry-standard containers and pallets. So, in addition to commerce-standard 88 x 125in, 108 x 125in, and 96 x 125in it can also accept LD-9, military pallets, demi LD-3, AEH and hazardous materials containers.

PEMCO also has a nine-position 'Alternate High Density' layout for the 737-400 with eight full-size 96 x 125in positions and one 88 x 125in position, and a combi option with four ULD positions in the forward cargo area for containers or pallets with a 25,000lb payload, and fixed seating for 66 or 72 passengers.

PEMCO has now redelivered more than 150 737-300s and 737-400s. As well as the Classic conversions, the company also has options for the

BELOW LEFT • *Designed to carry up to 52,800lb (23,949kg) on 2,023 nautical mile routes, the 737-800BCF offers 5,000 cu ft main deck capacity.* BOEING

BELOW RIGHT • *Since the start of 2020, Aeronautical Engineers has announced 26 orders for its 737 conversions from customers including Allied Air.* BOEING

BOTTOM • *West Atlantic in Sweden was the first 737-800BCF operator.* BOEING

business involved ten 737-400SFs, two 737-300SFs and 14 737-800SFs.

AEI has now received more than 90 orders for the 737-800SF since its 2015 launch. The first example, a 1999-vintage former Corendon Airlines jet, was delivered to its customer, the lessor GECAS, with Ethiopian Airlines subsequently leasing the jet.

Further proof of increased demand is AEI expanding its capabilities. In 2020 it has announced KF Aerospace in Canada and HAECO Xiamen as further 737-800SF conversion centres, taking to five the number of AEI conversion facilities for 737-800s. The others are Commercial Jet Inc in Miami, Florida, Commercial Jet Services in Dothan, Alabama, and the Shandong Aircraft Engineering Company (STAECO) in Shandong, China.

PEMCO Conversions

Other 737 conversions by third-party specialists are available. Tampa, Florida-based PEMCO Conversions offers

737-700. A full freighter conversion offers 3,844cu ft volume and 45,000lb payload with up to nine pallet positions - eight 88 x 125in or 88 x 108in pallets plus a smaller pallet.

A further 737-700 choice is FlexCombi, which offers three different configurations. These comprise a 24-passenger cabin and a 2,640 cu ft cargo hold with six pallet positions for 30,000lb payloads, a 12-passenger cabin and a 3,005 cu ft cargo hold for up to 35,000lb payloads in seven pallet positions, and full-freighter mode with a 3,370 cu ft cargo hold for up to 40,000lb payload in eight pallet positions.

All the configurations can accommodate 88 x 125in or 88 x 108in pallets, with the seventh and eighth positions accommodating smaller pallets. The FAA approved FlexCombi in July 2020.

IAI Bedek

IAI Bedek offers the 737BDSF (Bedek Special Freighter). In the IAI conversions, a new main deck smoke/fire detection and suppression system and a hydraulic main deck cargo door together with modified environmental control, water/waste, oxygen, and electrical systems are installed.

In March 2020, the US Federal Aviation Administration and Civil Aviation Authority of Israel awarded an STC for IAI's 737-800BDSF. According to IAI's data, the 737-800BDSF offers 53,000lb payload. Three different

configuration options are available, the first of which is 11 88 x 125in ULDs and one 79 x 60.4in. The second layout is for 11 ULDs sized at 88 x 108in and one 79in x 60.4in ULD. The third option is for nine 88 x 125in containers with either one smaller ULD or a single pallet.

The 737-800BDSF complements IAI's other converted 737 freighter conversion, the 737-700BDSF. The company says the 737-700BDSF has a 154,500lb MTOW, 129,200lb MLW and a 41,500lb payload. Three configurations are available. The first, Configuration A, is for ten positions (eight 88 x 125in, one 80 x 42in and one 88 x 78.9in). Configuration B has nine positions:

seven 96 x 125in, one 80 x 42in and one 88 x 78in. Lastly, Configuration C is for five 88 x 125in ULDs, one engine pallet, one 80 x 43in, and one 88 x 78.9in.

Boeing Converted Freighter

Conversions are not only offered by third-party specialists. Boeing launched its own 737-800BCF (Boeing Converted Freighter) in February 2016.

Designed to carry up to 52,800lb (23,949kg) on 2,023 nautical mile routes, the 737-800BCF offers 5,000 cu ft main deck capacity, and a further 1,540 cu ft in two lower-lobe compartments. The fuselage can carry 12 main-deck ULDs (11 88in x 125in

and one 53in x 88in), one more than the 737-400, offering 2,000nm range.

The US Federal Aviation Administration certified the 737-800BCF in April 2018. Work on the first conversion, involving 2004-vintage c/n 32740 for the 737-800BCF launch customer, GECAS, was completed by Boeing Shanghai Aviation Services in Shanghai. This is one of three Chinese conversion facilities for 737-800BCFs; the others are STAECO in Jinan and Guangzhou Aircraft Maintenance Engineering Company Limited (GAMECO).

Reregistered as G-NPTA, the converted jet was delivered by GECAS to West Atlantic at East Midlands Airport in April 2018, which received three more 737-800BCFs over the following year.

Boeing had secured 134 orders and commitments for 737-800BCFs by late September 2020, the latest date for which figures are available. Thirty-six had been delivered by that point, with ASL Airlines and SpiceJet other operators.

Rising Demand

There are a couple of reasons why demand for 737-800 conversion is rising. The 'feedstock' – that is to say, the supply of airframes with ownership/lease/operating costs and flying hours favourable for cargo conversion – of 737 Classics is diminishing as those aircraft age, while the newer 737NG airframe offers more fuel efficiency,

lower maintenance costs and greater availability of certified pilots.

In its brochure Boeing also notes its 737-800BCF conversion has an OEM warranty and access to fully-integrated manuals, spare parts and the company's support and services portfolio including solutions for fuel efficiency, aircraft health monitoring, optimised maintenance, and electronic flight bags.

Boeing predicts a healthy market for converted narrowbody airliners over the long term. In its latest 20-year World Air Cargo Forecast issued in November

2020, it predicts air cargo will grow by 4% per year by 2039, stimulating demand for 2,430 new freighters. It estimates more than 1,500 of these aircraft will be conversions, and of that number, 72% (1,080 jets) will be 737-sized conversions.

Coulson Aviation 737-300 Fireliner

Although most 737 conversions serve the air cargo market, some jets have been modified for a different purpose. Coulson Aviation in Canada has

TOP • *A Coulson Boeing 737-300 Fireliner demonstrating its drop capability.* COULSON AVIATION

ABOVE • *IAI engineers working on the first 737-800BDSF conversion.* IAI

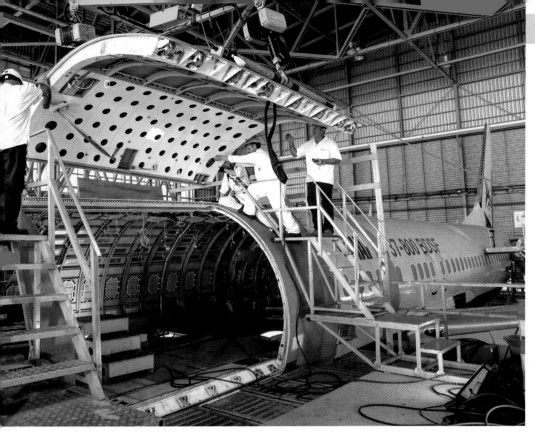

ABOVE • *Three different configuration options offering up to a 53,000lb payload are available on the 737-800BDSF.* IAI

All AEI-converted aircraft are re-designated as 737SFs. Modification work involves installing a cargo door on the left fuselage and modifying the main deck to a Class E cargo compartment. The cargo door is hydraulically operated and actuated. Hydraulic pressure for this system is available from a 28VDC electrically operated hydraulic pump or a manual hand pump.

converted several ex-Southwest Airlines 737-300s as aerial firefighters.

The company's conversion equips the aircraft with a 4,000 US gal tank able to carry water or retardant, and a new advanced delivery system called the RADS-XXL/2 specifically designed by Coulson for this application.

According to the company, 43,000 man-hours are required to complete the conversion, which involves installing the RADS-XXL/2 and a new 72-seat passenger cabin, avionics upgrades, and a full strip and re-paint.

The Fireliner modifications were designed, manufactured, and installed in house by the Coulson Group, which is the first company to convert a 737 as a firefighter.

The company says: "Once complete, the Fireliner is differentiated from all other Next Generation Large Airtankers by its ability to transport firefighters without re-configuration and to fly at maximum speeds and altitudes with a load of retardant and no restrictions."

The Fireliner has joined Coulson's diverse fleet of firefighting fixed-wing aircraft and helicopters, which range

from the sole airworthy Martin Mars to C-130 Hercules and CH-47 and UH-60 Helitankers.

Coulson completed the first Fireliner conversion on N137CG (c/n 27700, ex-Southwest N617SW) in 2017. This aircraft, aka Tanker 137, conducted its initial operational drops in July 2018

supporting firefighting efforts in San Bernardino, California.

Coulson Group CEO Britt Coulson commented: "The RADS-XXL/2 performed perfectly as did the airplane. Our flight crew couldn't have been happier with the handling characteristics and our split tank worked as designed with no centre of gravity shift during the drop."

Two other ex-Southwest 737s were subsequently modified as Fireliners by the company: N138CG (c/n 27928, previously N608SW, aka Tanker 138) and N139CG (c/n 28035).

In the 2018/19 Australian summer the New South Wales Government Rural Fire Service (NSWRFS) leased a Fireliner to support its bushfire fighting capabilities.

Subsequently, in May 2019, the agency acquired Tanker 138 from Coulson to provide its first year-round large air tanker capability. Now known as Bomber 210, this jet was repainted into a new colour scheme by Flying Colors Aviation in Townsville during 2020. It conducted its first missions of the 2020/21 bushfire season in October 2020 in both New South Wales and Victoria. The aircraft are operated by Coulson's Australian subsidiary.

NSW RFS acting commissioner Rob Rogers said the Service had evaluated different large air tankers over recent fire seasons and had settled on the 737 as the preferred option. Rogers said: "This type of aircraft provides us with a fast, effective and flexible option for fighting fires year-round, and supporting firefighters on the ground."

Separately, on November 6, 2020 the United States Forest Service awarded Coulson a five-year contract to provide 737 Fireliner aircraft to them.

RIGHT • *The 737-800 has joined IAI's roster of 737 conversions.* IAI

SUBSCRIBE
TO YOUR FAVOURITE MAGAZINE
AND SAVE

Today's Gateways To The World
Airports of the World is a bi-monthly magazine which provides an in-depth look at the layout, activities, aircraft, airlines and people at a wide selection of the world's airports. Reporting on airports large and small around the world, it includes articles on both major city hubs and smaller regional airports to leisure and low cost airports. Topics covered include current operations, airline operators, and future plans.

key.aero/airports-world

The Global Airline Scene
Published monthly, Airliner World is dedicated to bringing its readers the latest developments. It has a worldwide following comprising both industry readers and commercial aviation enthusiasts. For up-to-the-minute news and features on new leases, deliveries, technology, key industry personnel and airport developments from the airline scene; make Airliner World your magazine of choice!

key.aero/airliner-world

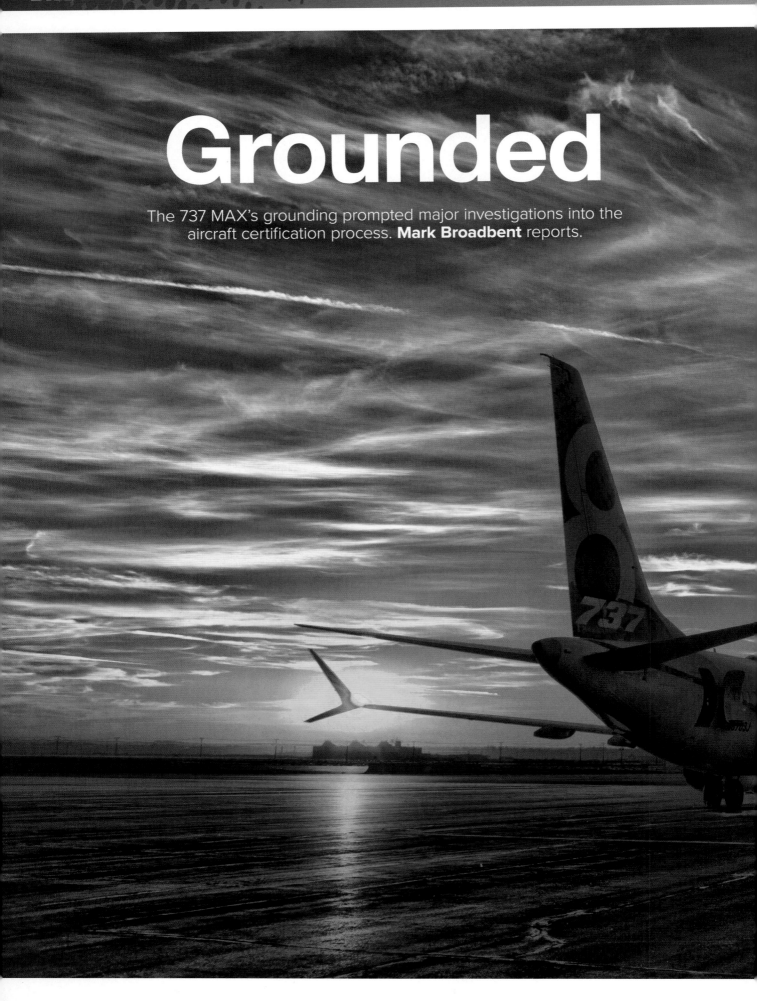

Grounded

The 737 MAX's grounding prompted major investigations into the aircraft certification process. **Mark Broadbent** reports.

On October 29, 2018, a Lion Air Boeing 737 MAX 8 operating Flight JT610 departed Soekarno-Hatta International Airport in Jakarta, Indonesia. It was bound for Depati Amir Airport in Pangkal Pinang. Thirteen minutes into the flight, the aircraft crashed into waters northeast of Jakarta, approximately 18nm off the island of Java, killing all 189 passengers and crew.

Emergency Airworthiness Directive (AD) 2018-23-51 was subsequently issued by the US Federal Aviation Administration requiring flight crews to use a revised runaway stabiliser operational procedure if they encountered certain conditions.

The Emergency AD was issued to all affected civil aviation authorities. It was an interim action, and further action was planned based on what the regulator, the US Federal Aviation Administration, and Boeing learned from investigating the accident.

On March 10, 2019, Ethiopian Airlines Flight 302 from Addis Ababa to Nairobi, Kenya crashed shortly after departure, killing all 157 aboard. The second complete loss of a 737 MAX and its passengers and crew within five months led to an immediate response by regulators worldwide.

China's Civil Aviation Administration and the Indonesia's Ministry of Transportation grounded the aircraft on March 11, 2019, an action followed the next day by the European Union Aviation Safety Agency and the US Federal Aviation Administration on March 13, 2019.

What is MCAS?

Investigations into the Lion and Ethiopian accidents identified the 737 MAX's Manoeuvring Characteristics Augmentation System (MCAS) as a common factor.

The Indonesian National Transportation Safety Committee's final report into Flight 610, published on October 25, 2019, found MCAS to be a contributing factor. A preliminary Ethiopian Civil Aviation Authority accident report into Flight 302 released on April 4, 2019, and

The FAA and other US bodies commissioned studies to evaluate the initial certification of the 737 MAX and the broader aircraft certification process. The FAA invited nine other civil aviation authorities to be a part of the Joint Authorities Technical Review, which assessed the certification of the 737 MAX.

a subsequent interim report issued on March 9, 2020, also concluded that MCAS was one of the factors in the Ethiopian crash.

The MCAS is a flight control law designed, Boeing says, "to enhance the pitch stability of the airplane." It is not, as some media outlets have described it, an 'anti-stall' system.

A function of the aircraft's Speed Trim System (STS), the MCAS was first introduced on the 737 Classics. Using input from two nose-mounted sensors measuring airspeed, altitude, and angle of attack (AOA), the MCAS automatically trims the horizontal stabilisers on the tail upwards, in manual flight with flaps up, when the system detects the aircraft is flying with an elevated AOA in situations when the aircraft is climbing aggressively or turning with a high angle of bank. The system makes pitch trim commands to the horizontal stabiliser to prevent the upward pitch of the aircraft becoming too steep.

Investigations into the Ethiopian and Lion accidents identified erroneous AOA data from a malfunctioning AOA sensor may have triggered the MCAS, which pitched down the nose of the aircraft despite crews' repeated attempts to disengage the system.

A further issue with MCAS identified by the accident investigations involved the AOA DISAGREE alert, designed to inform pilots of significant discrepancies between the information provided by the AOA sensors, warning flight crews when data from one sensor is incompatible with the other.

In a statement issued on April 29, 2019, Boeing said that the AOA DISAGREE alert was only enabled on 737 MAX aircraft in which the customers had selected it.

The statement said: "The disagree alert was intended to be a standard, stand-alone feature on MAX airplanes. However, the disagree alert was not operable on all airplanes because the feature was not activated as intended.

The disagree alert was tied or linked into the angle of attack indicator, which is an optional feature on the MAX. Unless an airline opted for the angle of attack indicator, the disagree alert was not operable."

In a subsequent May 5, 2019 statement, Boeing said it had identified this discrepancy in 2017, before the Lion Air accident. It said: "In 2017, within several months after beginning 737 MAX deliveries, engineers at Boeing identified that the 737 MAX display system software did not correctly meet the AOA Disagree alert requirements. The software delivered to Boeing linked the AOA Disagree alert to the AOA indicator, which is an optional feature on the MAX and the NG. Accordingly, the software activated the AOA Disagree alert only if an airline opted for the AOA indicator."

The statement continued: "When the discrepancy between the requirements and the software was identified, Boeing followed its standard process for

Investigations into the Lion Air and Ethiopian Airlines accidents identified the 737 MAX's Manoeuvring Characteristics Augmentation System as a common factor.

determining the appropriate resolution of such issues. That review, which involved multiple company subject matter experts, determined that the absence of the AOA Disagree alert did not adversely impact airplane safety or operation.

"Accordingly, the review concluded, the existing functionality was acceptable until the alert and the indicator could be delinked in the next planned display system software update.

"Approximately a week after the Lion Air accident, on November 6, 2018, Boeing issued an Operations Manual Bulletin (OMB), which was followed a day later by the FAA's issuance of an Airworthiness Directive (AD). In identifying the AOA Disagree alert as one among a number of indications that could result from erroneous AOA, both the OMB and the AD described the AOA Disagree alert feature as available only if the AOA indicator option is installed.

"Boeing discussed the status of the AOA Disagree alert with the FAA in the wake of the Lion Air accident. At that time, Boeing informed the FAA that Boeing engineers had identified the software issue in 2017 and had determined per Boeing's standard process that the issue did not adversely impact airplane safety or operation. In December 2018, Boeing convened a Safety Review Board (SRB) to consider again whether the absence of the AOA Disagree alert from certain 737 MAX flight displays presented a safety issue. That SRB confirmed Boeing's prior conclusion that it did not. Boeing shared this conclusion and the supporting SRB analysis with the FAA."

Reviews and Investigations
Boeing worked with regulators and customers to develop fixes to the 737 MAX's systems to safely return the aircraft to service. (see Return of the MAX).

The issues around MCAS and the AOA DISAGREE alert that were identified in the accident investigations in 2019 precipitated numerous reviews into the design and certification process for the aircraft.

The FAA and other US bodies commissioned studies to evaluate the initial certification of the 737 MAX and the broader aircraft certification process. The FAA invited nine other CAAs to be a part of the Joint Authorities Technical Review (JATR), which assessed the certification of the 737 MAX.

The FAA took into consideration all relevant findings of the JATR. It also convened a Joint Operations Evaluation Board (JOEB) with international partners from Canada, Europe, and Brazil to evaluate and report on pilot training needs. The FAA's Flight Standardization Board (FSB) reviewed JOEB training recommendations and incorporated them into the FAA's report.

The FAA also commissioned a Technical Advisory Board (TAB) to independently review Boeing's

proposed corrective actions and documentation. The TAB consisted of technical experts with no involvement in the initial certification of the 737 MAX.

The JATR published its findings and recommendations on October 11, 2019. As its report emphasised, the JATR was not convened to review details related to returning the 737 MAX to service. Its task was "to review the work conducted during the 737 MAX certification programme, to assess whether compliance was shown with the required applicable airworthiness standards related to the flight control system and its interfaces, and to recommend improvements to the certification process if warranted."

House Transportation and Infrastructure Committee

Separately, the House of Representatives Committee on Transportation and Infrastructure undertook an 18-month investigation into the 737 MAX. It released its findings on September 16, 2020 in a report, which said there were "serious flaws and missteps in the design, development and certification of the aircraft."

The Committee's 238-page report identified five central themes. First, production pressures on Boeing and the 737 MAX program to compete with Airbus' A320neo. Second, what the report called "fundamentally faulty assumptions about critical technologies on the 737 MAX, most notably with MCAS."

Third, what the House Committee called a "culture of concealment." Their report said: "Boeing withheld crucial information from the FAA, its customers, and 737 MAX pilots, including internal test data that revealed it took a Boeing test pilot more than ten seconds to diagnose and respond to uncommanded MCAS activation in a flight simulator, a condition the pilot described as "catastrophic". Federal guidelines assume pilots will respond to this condition within four seconds."

A fourth theme was what the report called "conflicted representation." It said: "The FAA's current oversight structure with respect to Boeing creates inherent conflicts of interest that have jeopardized the safety of the flying public. The report documents multiple instances in which Boeing employees who have been authorized to perform work on behalf of the FAA failed to alert the FAA to potential safety and/or certification issues."

A fifth theme was what the authors called "Boeing's influence over the FAA's oversight structure." It said: "Multiple career FAA officials have

BELOW • *Undelivered 737 MAX aircraft on the ground at Boeing Field.* AIRTEAMIMAGES/RYAN PATTERSON

RIGHT • *The MCAS uses input from two nose-mounted sensors measuring airspeed, altitude, and angle of attack.* BOEING/ANTHONY PONTON

documented examples where FAA management overruled a determination of the FAA's own technical experts at the behest of Boeing."

Peter DeFazio, the chair of the House committee, said: "Our report gives Congress a roadmap on the steps we must take to reinforce aviation safety and regulatory transparency, increase federal oversight, and improve corporate accountability to help ensure the story of the Boeing 737 MAX is never, ever repeated."

On September 16, 2020, Boeing responded to the House report with the following statement: "Boeing cooperated fully and extensively with the Committee's inquiry since it began. We have been hard at work strengthening our safety culture and rebuilding trust with our customers, regulators, and the flying public.

"Multiple committees, experts, and governmental authorities have examined issues related to the MAX, and we have incorporated many of their recommendations, as well as the results of our own internal reviews, into the 737 MAX and the overall airplane design process.

"The revised design of the 737 MAX has received intensive internal and regulatory review, including more than 375,000 engineering and test hours and 1,300 test flights. Once the FAA and other regulators have determined the MAX can safely return to service, it will be one of the most thoroughly scrutinised aircraft in history, and we have full confidence in its safety.

"We have also taken steps to bolster safety across our company, consulting outside experts and learning from best practices in other industries. We have set up a new safety organization to enhance and standardize safety practices, restructured our engineering organization to give engineers a stronger voice and a more direct line to share concerns with top management, created a permanent Aerospace Safety Committee of our Board of Directors as well as expanded the role of the Safety Promotion Center.

"We have learned many hard lessons as a company from the accidents of Lion Air Flight 610 and Ethiopian Airlines Flight 302, and from the mistakes we have made. We have made fundamental changes to our company as a result and continue to look for ways to improve. Change is always hard and requires daily commitment, but we as a company are dedicated to doing the work."

Changes to Certification

After the House Committee on Transportation and Infrastructure published its report, chair DeFazio, ranking members Sam Graves and Garret Graves, and Subcommittee on Aviation chair Rick Larsen, unveiled a comprehensive bill seeking to reform and improve the FAA certification and regulatory processes.

Named the 'Aircraft Certification Reform and Accountability Act', the 85-page bipartisan legislation features 27 different sections. The bill directs the FAA administrator to require certain safety

Aircraft On Ground, Production and Deliveries Pause

When the grounding was imposed, 376 examples of the 737 MAX had been delivered. Southwest Airlines had received more 737 MAX 8s than any other customer, with 34.

The grounding obviously meant operators no longer had the planned number of aircraft in their fleet and therefore the expected number of available seats. Carriers were forced to implement schedule revisions, work their remaining aircraft harder, and/or lease in capacity under aircraft, crew, maintenance, and insurance agreements.

Deliveries were paused and in April 2019 Boeing cut back output from 52 to 42 jets per month, resulting in dozens of 737 MAX aircraft being parked outside the Renton factory.

As the grounding continued Boeing eventually paused production entirely in January 2020, with the work only resuming in May 2020.

standards relating to aircraft. It covers new requirements for disclosing safety-critical information, reinforces protection for whistle-blowers, strengthens civil penalties for regulatory violations, and directs the FAA to set global standards to enhance pilot training.

The proposed legislation also authorises $27 million for each fiscal year from 2021 through to 2023 in new appropriations.

This will be used by the FAA to hire and maintain certification-related personnel such as engineers, safety inspectors, human factors specialists, software, technical and cybersecurity experts, and others.

Return of the
MAX

Mark Broadbent reports on the changes that have been
made to the 737 MAX ahead of the aircraft's return to service.

On November 18, 2020, the FAA rescinded the March 2019 grounding order on the 737 MAX through Airworthiness Directive 2020-24-02, paving the way for the aircraft to fly again.

The move followed extensive testing and comprehensive reviews of a package of updates to the aircraft's software, training, and maintenance developed by Boeing to address the causes and contributing factors involved in the Lion Air and Ethiopian Airlines accidents.

Test flights on a Boeing 737 MAX 7 test aircraft involving pilots from the FAA and other regulators took place during summer 2020 to review the updated software.

An FAA statement said: "The design and certification of this aircraft included an unprecedented level of collaborative and independent reviews by aviation authorities around the world. Those regulators have indicated that Boeing's design changes, together with the changes to crew procedures and training enhancements, will give them the confidence to validate the aircraft as safe to fly in their respective countries and regions."

Boeing Commercial Airplanes president and CEO, Stan Deal, commented: "The FAA's directive is an important milestone. We will continue to work with regulators around the world and our customers to return the airplane back into service worldwide."

Boeing CEO David Calhoun said: "We will never forget the lives lost in the two tragic accidents that led to the decision to suspend operations. These events and the lessons we have learned as a result have reshaped our company and further focused our attention on our core values of safety, quality and integrity."

Flight Control Law

Airworthiness Directive 2020-24-02 lays out the requirements for airlines to resume 737 MAX services, which cover the installation of software enhancements, completing wire separation modifications and conducting pilot training.

Aircraft must be updated with a revised flight control law that uses inputs from both angle of attack (AOA) sensors to activate the Manoeuvring Characteristics Augmentation System (MCAS), identified as the common link in the two accidents.

The AD explains that the updated control law compares the inputs from the two sensors and if those inputs differ by more than 5.5 degrees for a specified period of time, the Speed Trim System (STS), which includes MCAS, will be disabled for the remainder of the flight. The deactivation will be indicated on the flight deck via an AOA DISAGREE alert.

According to Boeing the AOA DISAGREE alert, "provides additional context for understanding the possible cause of air speed and altitude differences between the pilot's and first officer's displays." The new MCAS design "eliminates the need for time-critical pilot actions beyond normal pitch attitude control," the AD notes.

The document says: "The new flight control laws now permit only one activation of MCAS per sensed high-AOA event, and limit the magnitude of any MCAS command to move the horizontal stabilizer such that the

"The FAA's directive is an important milestone. We will continue to work with regulators around the world and our customers to return the airplane back into service worldwide." Boeing Commercial Airplanes president and CEO, Stan Deal

resulting position of the stabilizer will preserve the flight crew's ability to control the airplane's pitch by using only the control column.

"This means the pilot will have sufficient control authority without the need to make electric or manual stabilizer trim inputs. The new flight control laws also include flight control computer [FCC] integrity monitoring of each FCC's performance and cross-FCC monitoring, which detects and stops erroneous FCC-generated stabilizer trim commands (including MCAS)."

The AD mandates changes in the 737 MAX aircrew flight manual "to add and revise flight crew procedures to facilitate the crew's ability to recognise and respond to undesired horizontal stabilizer movement and the effects of a potential AOA sensor failure".

The display of an AOA DISAGREE alert indicating certain AOA sensor failures, or a significant calibration issue is mandated. Installing new FCC software display system software are other new requirements.

On hardware, a Service Bulletin issued on November 10, 2020 mandates new horizontal stabiliser trim wire routing installations. In FAQs about the 737 MAX updates published on its website Boeing says: "During the [FAA] review the team determined that some of the wiring associated with the system wasn't separated as far apart as required by

the FAA. All airplanes will be modified to meet this requirement before returning to service. In some cases, we will perform this task for our airline customers; in others, we'll provide them with all of the technical documentation and materials they need to do the work themselves."

The FAA requires an AOA sensor system test and an operational readiness flight on a jet with the upgraded software before the aircraft returns to service. Finally, the AD "only allows despatch of an aircraft with certain inoperative systems if specific, more restrictive, provisions are incorporated into the operator's existing FAA-approved minimum equipment list."

Safety Items

The rationale for all the actions in the AD is explained in greater depth in the FAA's 99-page Review of the Boeing 737 MAX, issued by the agency on November 18, 2020 along with the Airworthiness Directive.

According to this report, seven Safety Items were identified in the FAA's investigations:
1. Erroneous data from a single AOA sensor activating MCAS and subsequently causing nose-down trim

of the horizontal stabilizer.
2. When a continuous erroneous high AOA sensor value exists, the MCAS control law uses pilot release of the electric trim switch to reset MCAS activation.
3. Incremental commands for the MCAS moved the horizontal stabilizer a fixed amount, regardless of the current position of the stabilizer, which the flight crew could not counter using only elevator control.
4. Flight crews were unable to effectively manage the stabilizer movement and "flight deck effects" resulting from the single AOA sensor failure.
5. The AOA DISAGREE alert message on the primary flight display is not functional unless the AOA indicator option was chosen by the airline.
6. An extremely remote FCC failure condition required timely pilot intervention to ensure continued safe flight and landing.
7. Miscalibration of replacement AOA sensors.

Corrective Actions

The FAA report listed the corrective actions that have been undertaken to address each of these safety issues:

ABOVE • *The Boeing 737 MAX 7 was used in the FAA's flight testing.* BOEING

1. Boeing updated the FCC software to eliminate MCAS reliance on a single AOA sensor signal by using both AOA sensor inputs and changing flight control laws to safeguard against MCAS activation due to a failed or erroneous AOA sensor.

2. Boeing changed flight control laws to ensure MCAS will not command repeated movements of the horizontal stabilizer. The revised flight control laws permit only one activation of MCAS per sensed high-AOA event. Any subsequent activation of MCAS would only be possible after the airplane returns to a low-AOA state.

3. Boeing changed flight control laws to include a limit for MCAS commands. The MCAS will stop commanding stabilizer movement at a point that preserves enough elevator movement for sufficient pilot control of aircraft pitch attitude for current operating conditions.

4. In addition to the software changes noted in Safety Items #1, #2 and #3, Boeing revised or added eight non-normal flight crew procedures to the Airplane Flight Manual and proposed additional training. The flight crew procedures and the revised pilot training provide the pilot additional information to recognise and respond to erroneous stabilizer movement and the effects of potential AOA sensor failures.

5. Boeing has revised the AOA DISAGREE alert message implementation to achieve the original design intent to be standard on all 737 MAX aircraft.

6. Boeing implemented cross FCC Trim Monitor, which can effectively detect and shut down erroneous stabilizer commands from the FCCs. This makes continued safe flight and landing for this type of failure not dependent on pilot reaction time.

7. The Collins Component Maintenance Manual for the AOA sensor was revised to include a final independent check to ensure the repair has not introduced a bias. To ensure the two AOA sensors are functioning properly upon return to service, operators must perform AOA Sensor System Tests on each airplane prior to its return to service. This test uses a fixture to position the AOA vane and verify that the reading provided by each AOA sensor is accurate.

Flight Control Software Update

The FAA Review of the 737 MAX also disclosed that the aircraft will receive an additional software change that will provide further monitoring of the FCC and "provide additional protections against MCAS malfunctions or any other erroneous FCC-generated stabilizer trim command."

The change is intended to provide further support to address the Safety Item on stabiliser runaway failures, and additional protection against erroneous trim commands caused by "possible but unlikely" failures, such as a fault within a single integrated circuit in the FCC.

In its FAQs Boeing noted the runaway stabiliser fault "has never occurred during the 200 million hours of flight operations on any 737" but the new software "will be loaded on all airplanes before they return to service."

The FAA Return to Service document says: "The software update to both primary flight displays includes improved AOA DISAGREE annunciation logic, which addresses Safety Item #5: AOA DISAGREE alert message. The AOA DISAGREE annunciation is now always enabled, regardless of the AOA gauge option. An additional improvement locks the AOA DISAGREE annunciation when the aircraft is below 400 feet in altitude."

To reflect the various updates, Boeing proposed eight new or changed procedures in the Airplane Flight Manual (AFM): SPEED TRIM FAIL, Airspeed Unreliable, AOA DISAGREE, ALTITUDE (ALT) DISAGREE, Runaway Stabilizer, Indicated Airspeed (IAS) DISAGREE, Stabilizer Trim Inoperative, and STAB OUT OF TRIM. These changes, along with certain changes to training (see below) address Safety Item #4: FLIGHT CREW RECOGNITION AND RESPONSE.

The FAA Return to Service document says: "As a result of the design work to change the MCAS behaviour and the subsequent review of the Integrated Speed Trim System Safety Analysis, the FAA required an additional evaluation of the related aircraft systems for all flight phases and system modes.

"The FAA evaluated Boeing's determination of a non-compliance with FAA wire separation requirements. As a result, Boeing developed changes to the system, which include physical separation of existing wires and/or routing of new wires in multiple areas of the Main Electric Trim and Auto Trim system."

Training Enhancements

The 737 MAX Joint Operations Evaluation Board (JOEB) concluded evaluation activities at London Gatwick Airport on September 22, 2020. The JOEB included civil aviation authorities and airline crews from the United States, Canada, Brazil, and the European Union. The civil aviation authorities and industry pilots selected for participation completed all scheduled tasks as planned and, said the FAA, "the JOEB determined that all design changes applicable to the 737 MAX are 'operationally suitable'."

The JOEB evaluations also included assessments of Boeing's proposed differences in training and return to service training. Through evaluations of multiple crews, it determined the proposed training was 'acceptable'.

After considering public comments received, the FAA published the final version of the 737 Flight Standardization Board (FSB) report on November 18, 2020. This revision adds training requirements for the MCAS, Autopilot Flight Director System enhancements, and additional Special Emphasis Training.

The FAA's FSB and JOEB are to separately assess the effectiveness of the aircraft design changes on pilot training including evaluating all proposed flight crew procedure changes, in conjunction with other international civil aviation authorities.

In its FAQs Boeing says: "Boeing's training proposal includes a new suite

ABOVE • *Ryanair expects its 737 MAX 200 deliveries to begin early in 2021.* BOEING

RIGHT • *Boeing expects to deliver around half of the aircraft currently in storage by the end of 2021.* BOEING/MARIAN LOCKHART

of computer-based training modules, new and updated documentation, and simulator training. These instructional materials are designed to provide 737-type rated pilots with an improved understanding of 737 MAX flight control systems, reinforce their technical knowledge of associated flight deck effects and operational procedures, and restore confidence in the 737 MAX.

"We continue to work with regulators as they review the proposed training, and with our customers to understand their training needs and how we can continue to support them as we work to safely return the 737 MAX to service."

Return to Service

With the FAA's AD in place, US operators of the 737 MAX such as American Airlines and Southwest Airlines can now operate the type again, although obviously only after their aircraft receive the mandated corrective actions and pilots complete the new

training related to the revised MCAS.

The FAA's AD covers only 737 MAX aircraft registered with US operators, so the key to the 737 MAX operating globally will be other regulators authorising the jet to fly again. In its FAQs Boeing notes: "While the FAA's processes do inform other civil aviation authorities, we continue to work with these regulators as they take their own actions to return the airplane to service for their air carriers."

On November 25, 2020 the Brazilian regulator, ANAC, rescinded its AD that grounded commercial operations of 737 MAX 8s in Brazil.

The European Union Aviation Safety Agency (EASA) will parallel the software and technical requirements laid out by the FAA. It had yet to recertify the 737 MAX at the time of writing, but a November 24, 2020 Safety Directive noted EASA conducted a comprehensive review of the measures proposed by Boeing, including flight testing,

and considers the corrective actions "adequately address" the issues.

The European regulator's directive does include a couple of additional measures for European operators.

It states: "EASA has gathered factual evidence that, upon single failure of an AOA sensor during a Required Navigation Performance - Authorization Required (RNP-AR) approach, all flight guidance that allows the pilot to guide the aeroplane along the intended flight path is lost, and therefore the crew is left with no means to ensure that the aeroplane's trajectory can be maintained within the tolerated lateral deviation."

The directive said: "This condition, if not corrected, may constitute an unsafe condition in case the RNP-AR approach has been implemented because of terrain or obstacle constraints in the vicinity of the airfield. For the reasons described above, after the actions required by this SD have been accomplished, the affected Boeing 737-8 and 737-9 aeroplanes can be used...with the limitation not to perform RNP-AR approach operations.

"In order to ensure safe operation of the affected Boeing 737-8 and 737-9

"The design and certification of this aircraft included an unprecedented level of collaborative and independent reviews by aviation authorities around the world. Those regulators have indicated that Boeing's design changes, together with the changes to crew procedures and training enhancements, will give them the confidence to validate the aircraft as safe to fly in their respective countries and regions." Federal Aviation Authority

aeroplanes upon return to service, this SD requires that pilots perform the return to service training, including ground and flight training in a suitable full flight simulator, prior to operating the affected aeroplane."

Boeing has provided airlines whose 737 MAX aircraft have parked since the grounding was imposed in March 2019 with detailed recommendations regarding long-term storage. Operators must also ensure they take the required upgrade actions to fly again.

At the time of writing in November 2020, it was uncertain when the 737 MAX would return to airline service, although American Airlines had tentatively scheduled December 29, 2020 as the date for services to resume.

Resuming Deliveries

The build-up of completed airframes at Renton due to the length of the grounding means there is also a sizeable backlog of 737 MAXs to upgrade.

Speaking during Boeing's Q3 2020 earnings call on September 29, 2020, Boeing CEO Dave Calhoun said Boeing currently has "approximately 450 737 MAX aircraft built and stored in inventory."

He said: "We expect to have to remarket some of these aircraft and potentially reconfigure them, which will extend the delivery timeframe. We now expect delivery of about half of the aircraft currently in storage by the end of [2021] and the majority of the remaining in the following year. Delivery from storage will continue to be our priority after assisting our customers with their return to service."

Globally, new deliveries and the resumption of operations with jets already handed over also depends on the recertification of the aircraft by other regulators apart from the FAA.

During the airline's FY2021 first-half earnings call in November 2020, Ryanair CEO Michael O'Leary said the carrier expects to receive the first 737 MAX 200 delivery in late January or early February 2021.

Ryanair is the launch operator of the 737 MAX 200, the higher-capacity 737 MAX 8 subvariant, and hopes to take delivery of multiple aircraft in time for the summer 2021 schedule, with a target to take on 30 jets for the peak of the season.

Calhoun said Boeing expects 737 MAX delivery timings and the production rate profile to be "dynamic" and also noted it will also "ultimately be dictated by the pace of the commercial market recovery" from COVID-19.

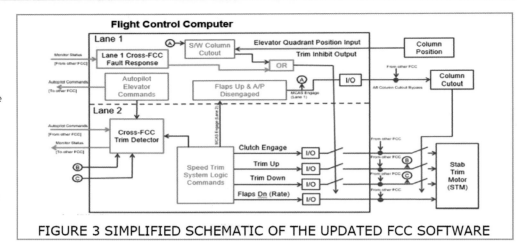

FIGURE 3 SIMPLIFIED SCHEMATIC OF THE UPDATED FCC SOFTWARE

ABOVE • *Schematic of the updated flight control computer software published in the November 2020 FAA report.* FEDERAL AVIATION ADMINISTRATION

BELOW • *Airworthiness Directive 2020-24-02 lays out the requirements for airlines to resume 737 MAX services covering software enhancements, wire separation modifications and pilot training.* BOEING/CHAD SLATTERY

The FAA Review of the 737 MAX disclosed that the aircraft will receive an additional software change that will provide further monitoring of the FCC and "provide additional protections against MCAS malfunctions or any other erroneous FCC-generated stabilizer trim command."

In Depth: MCAS

The November 18, 2020 US Federal Aviation Administration Review of the Boeing 737 MAX provided more detail about the Manoeuvring Characteristics Augmentation System (MCAS). Here, presented verbatim from the report, is an extract from the report detailing MCAS.

MCAS System Description and Flight Deck Effects

The originally certified design of the MCAS control law enabled the system to activate repeatedly during manual flight (Autopilot OFF) and when the flaps are fully retracted. Once enabled, and if the airplane's AOA exceeded a threshold, MCAS provided the potential for multiple activations of the MCAS automatic airplane nose-down stabilizer trim commands if the pilot used the main electric trim switch during the high-AOA event.

The new design changes this behavior. Boeing modified the flight-control-law logic to ensure that MCAS activation cannot be reset and command repeated movements of the horizontal stabilizer. During an activation MCAS can be paused if the pilots use the electronic trim switches. MCAS will resume after the switches are released but will only continue moving the horizontal stabilizer up to the maximum remaining command from the original activation appropriate for that airspeed. The revised flight control law logic will allow only one MCAS activation for each high-AOA event.

After the manual flight maneuver that created the high AOA and consequent single MCAS nose-down command, MCAS now makes an airplane nose-up (ANU) command to return the stabilizer to the pre-activation trim position upon returning to low AOA flight — if the pilot has not changed the trim.

If the pilot has changed the trim during the MCAS maneuver, MCAS will now return to the new reference stabilizer position set by the trim input. The MCAS flight-control law will be reset once the AOA falls sufficiently below the MCAS AOA threshold.

For example, in the original and the new versions, normal MCAS activation during manual flight would occur when the airplane is at a high AOA (such as during a high-speed tight-banked turn or low-speed approach to stall). During these maneuvers, the pilot may continue to pull back on the control column resulting in a higher AOA. To improve pitch stability, MCAS commands nose-down stabilizer. The result of the MCAS nose-down input makes the control column feel heavier as the pilot pulls back. This heavier feel complies with control-force requirements in FAA regulations.

After completing the tight turn and returning to level flight, the incremental stabilizer input made by MCAS during the high AOA condition is removed by MCAS.

The updated MCAS control law does not affect the attention, perception and reasonable decision making of the flight crew because there are no changes in flight deck effects in nominal MCAS activation scenarios. For certain potential AOA failures, such as physical failure due to damage or a mis-calibration, the updated FCC software reduces crew workload by inhibiting MCAS activation and presenting the SPEED TRIM FAIL alert (which has no associated crew tasks).

Section 6.1 describes Boeing's design and functional changes that address Safety Item #1: USE OF SINGLE AOA SENSOR, Safety Item #2: MCAS RESET GENERATES REPETITIVE MCAS COMMAND and Safety item #3: MCAS TRIM AUTHORITY.

6.1 System Description

Both the 737 NG and the 737 MAX include a Speed Trim System that automatically moves the horizontal stabilizer in response to changes from trimmed airspeed while in manual flight for speed stability. The 737 MAX includes an additional pitch augmentation flight control law called MCAS, which affects pitch characteristics in manual flight, with flaps up and at elevated angles of attack, to compensate for the aerodynamic pitch effects associated with the 737 MAX's larger, more forward located engines. MCAS enables the 737 MAX to comply with FAA regulatory requirements for certain handling qualities and cannot be removed unless replaced with a comparable system. Boeing has not presented a comparable system so the need for MCAS remains.

The MCAS flight-control law is part of the Speed Trim System and is commanded by the FCC using data from sensors and other airplane systems. As a stability-augmentation system, MCAS automatically makes commands without pilot action. Either pilot can override MCAS commands to control the stabilizer by using the electric stabilizer trim switches on the control wheel. Additionally, flight crews can set the STAB TRIM CUTOUT switches on the center control stand to CUTOUT to stop and disable MCAS.

The MCAS flight-control law becomes active when the airplane exceeds an AOA threshold that varies depending on Mach (airspeed). If activated by a high AOA, MCAS moves the horizontal stabilizer at a rate of 0.27 degrees per second, which is the same trim rate as Speed Trim with flaps down. The magnitude of the MCAS command is a function of Mach and angle of attack. At higher airspeeds, flight-control surfaces are more effective than at lower airspeeds. Therefore, a smaller MCAS command at higher airspeeds has the same effect as a larger MCAS command at lower speeds. At low Mach, when the stabilizer has lower effectiveness, the MCAS command can be up to the maximum of 2.5 degrees of incremental stabilizer movement. The MCAS flight control law is reset after the AOA falls sufficiently below the AOA threshold.

6.1.1 Overview of Updated MCAS Flight Control Laws

This section describes multiple updates within the MCAS function. The MCAS activation and resynchronization logic limits airplane nose-down stabilizer command during a single elevated AOA event. Once the AOA has been reduced, the system will return the stabilizer to a new reference trim position if the pilot activates electric trim while MCAS is making a command, which will account for any pilot trim input made during the MCAS command. An AOA split-vane monitor and middle-value select (MVS) have been added to prevent MCAS from using AOA inputs that differ from the other AOA input by more than 5.5 degrees. Boeing set the designed AOA input differential threshold of 5.5 degrees, based on electro-mechanical tolerances of the sensor and normal transient aerodynamic effects on the AOA sensors mounted on opposite sides of the fuselage during flight with flaps up. MVS logic has been added to the MCAS AOA signal processing to mitigate the potential hazard of undetected erroneous oscillatory AOA signal.

6.1.2 MCAS Activation/Resynchronization

During the original 737 MAX certification, Boeing demonstrated compliance with certain regulatory requirements for handling qualities by the functionality of MCAS. The airplane-level requirement to be compliant with those regulations remains, so the need for MCAS remains unchanged. The updated MCAS design retains the original MCAS activation thresholds for nominal conditions (i.e., absent sensor failures or pilot electric trim interaction). The revised MCAS activation criteria now include a requirement for the AOA to transition from a low AOA state (below the threshold) to a high AOA state (above the threshold) after the airplane is in the configuration and flight region where MCAS is utilized (flaps up and manual flight).

This single activation of MCAS will be limited to maximum of 2.5 degrees of airplane nose-down stabilizer motion (which is referred to as a single MCAS command). Reset of the MCAS system requires the AOA to transition sufficiently below the activation threshold. Since MCAS no longer resets after pilot activation of the electric trim switch, the five-second wait time following MCAS flight-control-law reset has been eliminated.

MCAS activation will be halted during the use of pilot electric stabilizer trim. Upon completion of the pilot's electric stabilizer trim inputs, MCAS may provide additional airplane nose-down stabilizer trim command if the AOA remains elevated and is continuing to increase. However, the airplane nose-down trim command cannot exceed a cumulative total of one MCAS delta stabilizer table value (maximum of 2.5 degrees as a function of Mach) for each high AOA event.

If pilot electric stabilizer trim is activated while above the AOA threshold, during the return to trim, MCAS would only command nose-up trim equivalent to the amount of nose-down trim that MCAS commanded following the last pilot electric trim input. This will move the stabilizer to the new reference trim position.

6.1.3 AOA Input Monitoring: Split Vane Monitor and Middle Value Select (MVS)
In the new design, each FCC receives left and right AOA sensor values from the left and right Air Data Inertial Reference Unit (ADIRU), respectively. The AOA values are transmitted from the ADIRUs to the FCCs via databuses.

During normal operation, accurate AOA values are transmitted over the databuses with a label that the values are considered "valid" by the ADIRU.

The AOA sensor electrical circuit includes wiring within the AOA sensor and wiring between the sensor and the ADIRU. A failure of that electrical circuit (e.g., open, short, etc.) will be detected by the ADIRU, and the ADIRU will not transmit data on the bus as being "valid."

This failure scenario is referred to as a "detected failed" condition.

Certain AOA sensor failures are not related to degradation of the electrical circuit, and therefore are not detected by the ADIRU. These failures result in AOA values transmitted by the ADIRU as "valid" when, in fact, they are not correct. These outputs of the ADIRU are referred to as "valid erroneous" data. Examples of failures that result in erroneous data include a bent or broken AOA vane (e.g., due to a bird strike or ramp damage) or a mis-calibrated AOA sensor (e.g., JT610 scenario).

Each FCC receives and monitors the two AOA sensor inputs from the ADIRUs and determines which AOA value to use in the MCAS control-law calculations. AOA values are compared to one another by a split vane monitor and sent through a MVS algorithm.

The split vane monitor compares two valid AOA inputs and will use them only if the difference between the AOA values is less than or equal to 5.5 degrees. If the difference is greater than 5.5 degrees for a specified duration, the MCAS and Speed Trim functions will be disabled for the remainder of the flight. The split vane monitor becomes active after the flaps have been retracted during flight.

If the two valid signals are within the limits of the split vane monitor, they are put through the MVS algorithm. The MVS output is initialized at zero degrees. The MVS utilizes three numbers: the two current AOA values and the MVS output from the previous MVS determination. The algorithm determines the middle value of the three numbers by eliminating the highest and lowest values and using the remaining value (for example, for inputs 1, 2, and 4, the middle value is 2). The MVS algorithm is effective at minimizing the effect of a low amplitude oscillatory input value. The output of the MVS is used by the MCAS function within the FCC.

Effect of Erroneous AOA Value on MCAS — if the valid AOA value differs from the other valid AOA sensor value by more than 5.5 degrees for a specified duration the AOA values are considered erroneous, the split vane monitor will detect the failure and both the MCAS and Speed Trim functions will be disabled for the remainder of the flight. Activation of the split vane monitor will completely disable the STS (which includes both MCAS and Speed Trim System), will trigger a Master Caution indication, an illumination of the Flight Control (FLT CONT) annunciator, and an illumination of the SPEED TRIM FAIL light on the overhead panel. The Master

Caution indication and the FLT CONT annunciator can be reset by pressing the MASTER CAUTION PUSH TO RESET button. The SPEED TRIM FAIL light will remain illuminated for the remainder of the flight. In addition, an accompanying maintenance item is recorded for the loss of MCAS and Speed Trim. The SPEED TRIM FAIL annunciation is shown in Figure 2.

Effect of Detected Failed AOA Sensor on MCAS — if a failed AOA circuit is detected, the FCCs will receive only one valid AOA value. The FCCs will utilize the valid AOA value to control MCAS. The Split Vane Monitor and MVS are not utilized.

During execution of the descent phase Master Caution recall checklist procedure, the SPEED TRIM FAIL light will be illuminated so the pilots will be aware of the condition. MCAS and Speed Trim will continue to operate using the available valid AOA signal. This design preserves the availability of Speed Trim and MCAS operation after a single detected failed AOA sensor.

A second independent failure during the same flight is considered to be extremely improbable. If a second independent failure affects the remaining AOA sensor, any resulting activation of MCAS would be limited to a single MCAS command (up to 2.5 degrees as a function of Mach).

6.1.4 Forward Column Cutout Interaction
It is possible for the forward column cutout switch to be activated while the pilot is pushing the control column forward during recovery from an elevated AOA condition. If MCAS is providing an airplane nose-up trim command to return the stabilizer to the trim position, activation of the forward column cutout switch will pause the stabilizer movement.

The forward column cutout interaction change accounts for the time during which the stabilizer is not moving due to column cutout. It finishes making the ANU trim command when the command is not being cutout, thus improving the precision with which MCAS returns the stabilizer to the trim position.

6.1.5 MCAS Maximum Command Limit
This change limits the total amount of airplane nose-down stabilizer movement MCAS can command if there are repeated MCAS activations. This ensures that the flight crew will always have maneuver capability through control column inputs alone, enabling the flight crew to maintain level flight without requiring use of the electric trim switches or the stabilizer trim

cutout switches.

The redesigned FCC software compares the current stabilizer position to the stabilizer position that existed at initial MCAS activation. If the difference reaches a limit value that has been determined to preserve a maneuver capability with control column alone, then MCAS and Speed Trim operations are disabled for the remainder of the flight.

Flight crew intervention is not required to activate the MCAS Maximum Command Limit or to disable the MCAS and Speed Trim operations. As discussed previously, when MCAS and Speed Trim are disabled, SPEED TRIM FAIL is annunciated, and a maintenance item is recorded. Due to the MCAS changes previously discussed, this command limit is not expected to be used but provides an additional level of safety.

The maximum command-limit-reference-stabilizer position is reset by the FCC after one consecutive minute of the autopilot being engaged, or five consecutive minutes of manual flight below the MCAS AOA activation threshold, whichever comes first.

6.1.6 MCAS Engage and Stabilizer Trim Integrity Monitoring

MCAS Engage logic is computed in the FCC Lane 2 Central Processing Unit (CPU) and is communicated to the Lane 1 CPU. Lane 1 transmits the MCAS Engage signal which allows the FCC stabilizer trim to bypass the aft column cutout switch and sets the STM to run at the flaps-down FCC rate. In the updated FCC software, the Lane 1 CPU would only transmit MCAS Engage (as computed by the Lane 2 CPU) if the autopilot or Control Wheel Steering (CWS) are not engaged and the flaps are up. The purpose of this change is to reduce the likelihood of transmitting an erroneous MCAS Engage logic signal due to a Lane 2 CPU failure.

In addition, the updated FCC software replicates the mechanical column cutout functions using software. The Lane 1 CPU will inhibit transmittal of FCC Trim Up and Trim Down commands by the Lane 2 CPU if the commands are in opposition to the elevator surface position by an amount greater than that of the mechanical control column cutout switches. The Trim Down command will not be inhibited when the Lane 1 MCAS Engage discrete is True.

The magnitude of the software-column-cutout thresholds was set to a value outside the mechanical-control-column-cutout switches so it will not interfere with the mechanical switches while remaining effective if the mechanical switch fails to activate.

6.2 Cross-FCC Trim Monitor

The Cross-FCC Trim Monitor is a new feature to address Safety Item #6: OTHER POSSIBLE FCC STABILIZER RUNAWAY FAILURES and provides additional protection against erroneous FCC trim commands caused by postulated failures in the FCC Lane 2 CPU or I/O chips. This monitor is implemented in Lane 2 of the FCC.

While the FCCs are powered, each FCC continuously monitors the other FCC channel, except during dual-channel autopilot operation or when a Fail-operational configured airplane is performing an Autoland or automatic Go-Around. The FCC channel in which the autopilot or CWS is engaged, or which is the STS selected channel, is referred to as the operational FCC channel. The other FCC channel is referred to as the standby FCC channel.

The monitor compares the trim-up and trim-down command outputs from both FCCs with its own trim command calculation. The operational channel performs its normal stabilizer trim-command calculations for use by the monitor. The standby channel switches its data sources to use the same data as the operational channel to perform its stabilizer-command calculations for use by its monitor.

The following discussion applies to either the operational or standby channel:

If the stabilizer trim discrete outputs differ from the trim-command calculation in the local channel's monitor for a cumulative one second, as determined by an up/down counter, then the local channel will take control of STS (if it does not already have it) and send a discrete to Lane 1 of the foreign channel, indicating that the monitor has tripped. This will cause Lane 1 of the foreign channel to prevent transmittal of the foreign channel's Lane 2 stabilizer trim discrete outputs. If able, Lane 2 of the foreign channel will then set a SPEED TRIM FAIL discrete that will be observed during pilot execution of the descent phase Master Caution recall checklist procedure as described earlier in this section.

If the foreign channel's autopilot or CWS is engaged when the local channel's Lane 2 monitor has tripped, the autopilot or CWS will disconnect, accompanied by the autopilot disconnect warning aural and visual indications. Further attempts to engage the foreign channel's autopilot or CWS will be inhibited. Autopilot and CWS operation may still be available via the local channel.

In addition to the above, both channels will set the NO AUTOLAND discrete, causing NO AUTOLAND to be enunciated for the fail-operational configured airplanes. The channel whose monitor has tripped will also set the STAB OUT OF TRIM light to illuminate when on ground and below 30 knots. Illuminating the STAB OUT OF TRIM light on the ground ensures there is a maintenance action in the event the failed FCC channel is unable to report itself as failed using the SPEED TRIM FAIL light.

Cross-channel signals are added to ensure the Standby FCC is in MCAS operation any time the Operational FCC is in MCAS operation, reducing the number and duration of trim inhibits due to stab trim voting. The Standby FCC performs a reasonableness check on the Operational FCC signal to activate MCAS to ensure the activation difference is not due to a postulated FCC failure.

During Boeing research and development flight testing of the 737 MAX's updated software, a STAB OUT OF TRIM light illuminated on the forward instrument panel. Boeing determined that the illumination of this light was caused by differences in input data between the FCCs. Boeing revised the proposed final FCC software to ensure that this indicator light only illuminates as intended.

To reduce nuisance trips of the Command Response Monitor due to stab-trim voting logic, the Standby FCC stabilizer-trim calculations have been aligned further by using Operational FCC elevator commands directly. The Command Response Monitor sets the STAB OUT OF TRIM light while autopilot is engaged. An additional monitor, the Autopilot Elevator Command Integrity Monitor, was added to ensure the integrity of using the elevator command signal in the Standby FCC stabilizer trim calculations, which can be corrupted by postulated FCC Lane 1 failures.

A power-up test was added to the FCC software to verify the availability of the FCC hardware switches used by the Cross-FCC Trim Monitor to disable the Lane 2 stabilizer trim discretes and also check for the external trim wraparounds used by the Cross-FCC Trim Monitor to detect trim outputs of the other FCC. This test runs on power-up and after every landing.

Mid-Size

Turbofan

Chris Kjelgaard details the CFM International LEAP-1B engine

Although just one of three versions of CFM International's new LEAP mid-sized turbofan engine, the LEAP-1B powering all Boeing 737 MAXs will almost certainly be the most-produced version of the fastest-selling commercial-turbofan engine in history.

By the end of 2019, eleven years after CFM had launched design and development of the LEAP family, CFM — a joint venture between GE Aviation and Safran Aircraft Engines — had won firm orders and other commitments for more than 17,000 LEAP engines.

LEAP-1B Testing and Certification

Ground testing of the first LEAP-1B began on June 13, 2014, at Safran Aircraft Engines' test facility at Villaroche near Paris. The programme involved 12 LEAP-1B development engines, tests being performed both in France and the United States.

The LEAP-1B flew for the first time on April 29, 2015, installed on GE Aviation's Boeing 747 flying testbed. By this point, CFM had started building 'compliance' engines, configured to a standard suitable for type certification. The next major event in the LEAP-1B flight-test programme came on January 29, 2016, when the first 737 MAX 8, powered by two LEAP-1B compliance engines, performed its first flight.

On May 4, the Federal Aviation Administration, and the European Union Aviation Safety Agency each

So complex is the layering of the carbon fibre strands within in each fan blade that it allows each fan blade to untwist in a specific, controlled way as the blade rotation rate varies, modifying the blade's aerodynamic characteristics to provide optimal propulsive efficiency during different phases of flight.

awarded type certificates to the LEAP-1B, allowing 737 MAX 8 flight testing to continue. Type certificates were simultaneously awarded by the FAA and the EASA in May 2016 followed by service entry with Malaysian airline Malindo Air in May 2017.

CFM's production plans called for it to manufacture 2,000 LEAP engines of all versions by 2020, subsequently increased to as many as 2,200 a year.

Not only are these the highest annual production rates ever planned by any manufacturer of commercial aircraft turbofan engines, but they also involve by far the most intensive production ramp-up.

LEAP-1B Differences vs Other LEAP Versions

Like its sister engines the LEAP-1A and LEAP-1C (both of which are identical internally, but differ from the LEAP-1B),

the LEAP-1B incorporates a number of commercial turbofan technological firsts. In the LEAP-1B's case, these advances are intended to allow a fuel efficiency improvement of 15% over its predecessor, the 737NG's CFM56-7B, and despatch reliability of 99.98% – a rate as high as that which the CFM56 family, legendary for operational reliability, has achieved over 30 years of service.

However, no LEAP engine will share any part number in common with any CFM56; the LEAP is an entirely new design. Nor does the LEAP-1B share many part numbers with its sister LEAP engines. It has a smaller fan diameter, a slightly smaller core diameter, one fewer fuel-injection nozzle and two fewer low-pressure turbine (LPT) stages than the other two LEAP versions.

The LEAP-1B, designed for a 23,000lb–28,000lb thrust range rather than the 24,500lb–35,000lb range of the other two versions, has a 69.4in fan diameter, compared to the 78in fan diameter of the LEAP-1A and LEAP-1C. Its smaller fan diameter means the LEAP-1B's design bypass ratio is lower than that of the other two engines: 9:1 vs 11:1.

Boeing's requirement for a lower thrust range and a smaller fan diameter meant CFM could dispense with two of the seven LPT stages the other two LEAP versions boast.

LEAP-1B Engine Architecture and Fan

CFM aimed to achieve these qualities in its LEAP engines by incorporating new technologies, at the same time making each LEAP engine bigger and more complex than the relatively simple CFM56 designs. Behind the fan, each LEAP engine has a three-stage, low-pressure compressor (LPC), a ten-stage high-pressure compressor (HPC), a new 'TAPS II' combustor (the LEAP-1A and LEAP-1C's combustors each having 19 fuel-injection nozzles, but the smaller LEAP-1Bs 18), two high-pressure turbine (HPT) stages and seven LPT stages (five in the LEAP-1B).

One major technological advance in the LEAP-1B is its fan. For the first time in any commercial-aircraft engine as small as the mid-size LEAP, the entire fan, including all 18 blades, is made of carbon fibre. Not only does this make the fan assembly much lighter than a conventional metal fan would be, but it also makes it much stronger.

Made by Safran Aircraft Engines at facilities in France and New Hampshire, all LEAP fan blades are of what GE Aviation calls fifth-generation carbon fibre blade design. Previous generations began with ✈

ABOVE • BOEING

RIGHT • *The first LEAP-1B engine to test.* ALL PHOTOS CFM INTERNATIONAL UNLESS STATED

LEFT • *Each LEAP fan blade contains 4.35 miles of carbon fibre strands, and each strand is made up from many interwoven, individual carbon fibre filaments.*

the original GE90 and continued through the GE90-115B and the GEnx.

Manufactured using a technique called woven resin transfer moulding, each LEAP fan blade is made up of complex layers of carbon fibre strands. These are woven on gigantic Jacquard looms into a three-dimensional, aerodynamically efficient aerofoil and then are strengthened by impregnation with resin.

So complex is the layering of the carbon fibre strands that it allows each fan blade to untwist in a specific, controlled way as the blade rotation rate varies, modifying the blade's aerodynamic characteristics to provide optimal propulsive efficiency during different phases of flight. Each strand is made up from many interwoven, individual carbon fibre filaments.

Debris Rejection System and Combustor

Another technological advance in the LEAP design is a debris rejection system located between the LPC and HPC modules. Adopted from GE Aviation's GE90 design, this consists of eight variable-bleed valve doors that, upon engine spool-up, open automatically inward into the core airstream. These doors deflect all sand and other foreign-object debris out into the bypass airstream before it enters the core, preventing any foreign object debris from damaging the HPC stages' 3-D aerofoils.

Next as a technological advance is the highly aerodynamically optimised HPC module, which produces about half of the LEAP's overall efficiency improvement compared with the CFM56. The first five stages of the ten-stage HPC are one-piece blisks, reducing parts count and weight and improving durability. The HPC module generates a 22:1 pressure ratio, creating an overall pressure ratio of 40:1 from the fan to the combustor at take-off power.

The TAPS II combustor is particularly notable in that each fuel injection nozzle is made by an additive manufacturing process that uses a laser to melt metal powder into a liquid spray that is then deposited a layer at a time on to the preceding layer.

CMCs and Cooling-Air Advances

Yet another new technology in LEAP engines is the use of ceramic matrix composites (CMCs) in the first-stage HPT shroud, for the first time in any commercial engine. Ringing the first HPT rotating stage, this shroud is made from 36 interlocking CMC parts that are

The LEAP-1B has 18 fuel-injection nozzles.

BELOW • *The use of ceramic matrix composites in the first-stage high-pressure turbine shroud is a first in any commercial engine.*

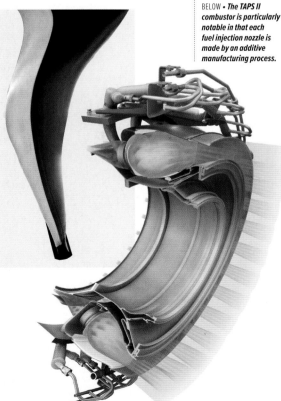

LEFT • *A computer-generated image of a LEAP engine.* GE AVIATION

BELOW LEFT • *Manufactured using a technique called woven resin transfer moulding, each LEAP fan blade is made up of complex layers of carbon fibre strands.*

BELOW • *The TAPS II combustor is particularly notable in that each fuel injection nozzle is made by an additive manufacturing process.*

not only much lighter than traditional metal alloy parts, but also require very little cooling, where alloy parts would need complex cooling-air circuits and lots of cooling air bled from the HPC.

Reducing this requirement has allowed CFM to use bleed air from the HPC more efficiently. One key use has been to provide cooling-air circuits to the HPT casing, the cooling air acting to increase the clearance between the HPT stages and the casing during low-thrust operations, increasing engine efficiency.

Another technology CFM has introduced in the LEAP — for the first time in any commercial engine — is to modulate, by means of the FADEC 4 software controlling the engine's operation, the amounts of bleed-air cooling going to the HPT stages' cooling-air circuits during different phases of flight.

The HPT stages need much more cooling air when the engine is operating at maximum thrust during take-off and initial climb than they do during low-thrust cruise and descent. By modulating the amounts of bleed air used for HPT cooling, CFM has further increased LEAP efficiency.

AVIATION SPECIALS

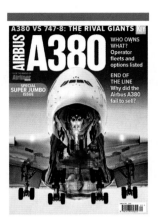

C-40
Clipper

The US Air Force and the US Navy currently operate a military airlift variant of the 737 dubbed the C-40 Clipper. **Tom Kaminski** reports

C-40C 09-0540, the fourth C-40C assigned to the 932nd Airlift Wing, taxis at its home station, Scott Air Force Base, Illinois. US AIR FORCE/TSGT DAN OLIVER

The US military received its first Boeing 737s in September 1973, when the initial examples of the 737-200 series airliner entered service. They were taken on roster with the US Air Force's 323rd Flying Training Wing (FTW) as navigational trainers at Mather Air Force Base, California. Assigned the designation T-43A, the aircraft first flew on March 10, 1973 and served in that role until the last examples were retired in September 2010. In addition to serving as navigational trainers, six of the 19 navigators were converted for airlift missions under the designation CT-43A and served with active-duty and Air National Guard units. One aircraft was written off in an April 1996 crash in Croatia that killed 35 personnel including the US secretary of commerce. In later years, three additional T-43As were converted to airliner configuration and operated by defence contractor EG&G in support of operations at the Area 51 Test Facility in Nevada. The last T-43As, assigned to the 12th FTW at Randolph Air Force Base, Texas, were retired in September 2010.

In the Navy

Naval Air Systems Command (NAVAIR) issued a formal request for proposals (RFP) associated with the purchase of a Navy Unique Fleet Essential Airlift Replacement Aircraft (NUFEA-RA) in April 1997. It was intended as a replacement for the service's fleet of 15 C-9B and 12 DC-9 series Skytrain II aircraft that operated in the medium lift intra-theatre transport role. Although still viable, the C-9Bs and DC-9s no longer met noise requirements and their avionic systems were rapidly becoming outdated. The aircraft were operated by five of the Naval Reserve's 11 Fleet Logistics Support Squadrons, abbreviated as VR. The VR squadrons provide 100% of the Navy's organic intra-theatre logistics airlift capacity. As part of their domestic and international operations, the squadrons conduct rotational deployments at Bahrain International Airport, Bahrain, Naval Air

Station Sigonella, Italy, and Naval Air Facility Atsugi, Japan in support of the US Fifth, Sixth and Seventh Fleets.

The NUFEA provides the fleet with world-wide short-notice, fast response intra-theatre logistics support. Two additional C-9Bs were operated in the operational support airlift role by the US Marine Corps. The Boeing 737-700C was chosen over Boeing's MD-90-30ER, which was based on the earlier DC-9 and was also offered by Boeing.

On August 29, 1997, NAVAIR awarded Boeing an $111 million contract covering the purchase of two 737-700C Increased Gross Weight Quick Change series aircraft. The -700C (Convertible) was launched in September 1997, following receipt of the US Navy order. It was based on the Boeing Business Jet 1 airframe, but modifications incorporated an 11 x 7ft forward cargo door, a new cargo handling system, an integrated aft air stair, and the ability to operate

> *The C-40A aircraft was certified to operate in an all-passenger, all-cargo variant or combi configurations. The three configurations allow the aircraft to alternately carry up to 121 personnel, 36,000lb of cargo on eight pallets or up to 15,000lb of cargo on three pallets and 70 passengers on the main deck.*

at an increased gross weight of up to 171,000lb. Powered by two GE Aviation CFM56-7B24 high bypass turbofan engines each rated at 24,200lb, the aircraft has a maximum range of 3,200nm and can operate at altitudes as high as 41,000ft. Based on the Boeing 777's flight deck, the aircraft's advanced digital cockpit features an electronic flight instrument system that includes five flat-panel displays, a dual flight management computer system with integrated GPS, reduced vertical separation minimum capability, traffic collision avoidance, enhanced ground proximity warning, and predictive

wind shear systems as well as a head-up display and TACAN/UHF/IFF functions. When delivered, the aircraft were compatible with future air traffic management operating environments.

Considered to be a commercial-off-the-shelf procurement, the 737-700C received type certification from the Federal Aviation Administration on August 31, 2002. In addition to being purchased using commercial best practices the fleet is maintained in accordance with an FAA-approved maintenance plan. Heavy maintenance for the C-40A fleet is currently carried out by AAR Corporation under a five-

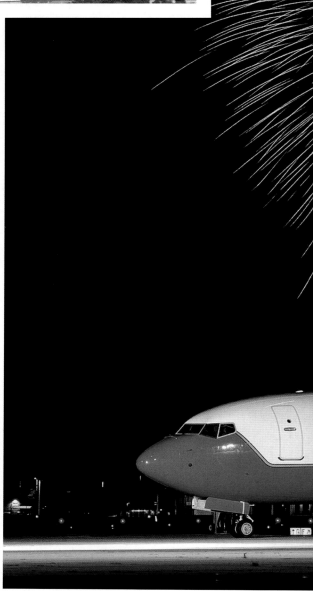

year, $104.9 million contract awarded in March 2016. The work is carried out at AAR's Maintenance, Repair and Overhaul facility at Will Rogers World Airport in Oklahoma City, Oklahoma.

Assigned the designation C-40A, the aircraft was certified to operate in an all-passenger, all-cargo variant or combi configurations. The three configurations allow the aircraft to alternately carry up to 121 personnel, 36,000lb of cargo on eight pallets or up to 15,000lb of cargo on three pallets and 70 passengers on the main deck. Although the early C-40As were delivered without winglets, the devices were installed on the ninth (BuNo 166693) and subsequent aircraft and retrofitted to the earlier aircraft. The winglets reduced drag by 5-7%, which improved fuel efficiency by 5.9%, boosted range by 150nm and increased the load by 6,000lb.

The C-40A first flew when BuNo 165829 carried out its initial flight from Renton Municipal Airport, Washington, on April 14, 1999. Following a series of test flights, it was ferried to Boeing's Wichita, Kansas, facility where cargo modifications were incorporated. It was formally unveiled at Boeing Field in Seattle on September 9, 2000. The first two C-40As were delivered to VR-59 'Lone Star Express' at Naval Air Station, Fort Worth Joint Reserve Base, Texas on April 21, 2001. The squadron had concluded C-9B operations earlier in October 2000. The first of three examples was assigned to VR-58 'Sunseekers' at Naval Air Station Jacksonville, Florida, on March 28, 2002 and the squadron accepted the last of the

initial six Clippers on October 28, 2002. VR-57 'Conquistadors' at Naval Air Station North Island, California, flew its final C-9B sortie in March 2005 and transitioned to the C-40A in August of that year.

VR-56 'Globemasters' followed and its transition to the C-40A began in May 2011. The squadron's first Clipper arrived at Naval Air Station Oceana, Virginia, on March 2, 2012, following its transfer from VR-57.

At Naval Air Station Whidbey Island, Washington, VR-61 'Islanders' retired the last US Navy Skytrain II on June 29, 2014, and the squadron's first C-40A arrived on November 21, 2014. Transition of the final squadron was completed on July 26, 2019, when VR-51 'Windjammers' received its second Clipper at Marine Corps Air Station Kaneohe Bay, Hawaii. The 'Windjammers', which previously operated the C-20G variant of the Gulfstream IV, had accepted its first aircraft earlier in May 2019.

Delivery of the 17th and final new-build C-40A to VR-57 occurred on October 23, 2019. Although the service's full requirement includes 23 aircraft, the delivery of BuNo 169793 to North Island completed the Navy's base requirement. An almost year-long grounding of the Navy's C-130T fleet that began in 2017 caused the service to rely heavily on its Clippers, which operated at maximum capacity to compensate for the loss of lift capability and capacity.

The initial group of five C-40As was funded under National Guard and Reserve Equipment Appropriations, and the subsequent ten were funded as congressional add-ons to the respective National Defense Authorization Acts. A final pair of Naval Clippers was authorized as part of a supplementary budget in FY2017.

Marine Clippers

The US Marine Corps operated a pair of C-9Bs until April 2017 when the Skytrain IIs assigned to Marine Transport Squadron 1 (VMR-1) 'Roadrunners' were finally retired and stored at the Mojave Air & Space Port in California. The squadron, which had been stationed at Marine Corps Air Station Cherry Point, North Carolina, later relocated to Naval Air Station Joint Reserve Base Fort Worth, Texas, in December 2017, in a move that coincided with its transition from the active-duty Marine Corps to the Marine Corps Reserve. Since relocating to Texas, VMR-1 has been sharing the responsibility for C-40As assigned to the US Navy's VR-59, while it awaits its own Clippers. Under the terms of a two-year, $118.6 million contract awarded by the US Navy in July 2019, AAR Government Services will acquire two Boeing 737-700 (IGW) series aircraft and modify them to the C-40A configuration. Funded by the 2018 National Defense Authorization Act, the pre-owned 737s will be delivered to VMR-1 in Fort Worth by September 2021.

BELOW • *C-40C 05-0730 assigned to the 932nd Airlift Wing at Truax Field, Madison, Wisconsin during a firework display to mark Independence Day.* US AIR FORCE RESERVE COMMAND/JOE OLIVA

Air Force Variants

The US Air Force operates a fleet of 11 737-700 series BBJs under the designations C-40B and C-40C Clippers. Four C-40Bs are assigned to Air Mobility Command's 89th Airlift Wing, and seven C-40Cs are operated by Air Force Reserve Command and Air National Guard and are 'gained' by Air Mobility Command. The C-40B is based on the 737-7DM and 737-7FD (BBJ1). Like the C-40A, it features the 737-800's strengthened wing and landing gear, but it is not equipped with a cargo door or handling equipment. Designed to be an 'office in the sky' for senior military and government

leaders, the C-40B features a crew rest area equipped with four business-class seats, dual communications system operator stations, a conference/staff area with eight business-class seats and work tables, and a distinguished visitor compartment with sleep area, two business-class seats and a workstation. Communications capabilities provide broadband data/video transmit and receive capability and secure and non-secure voice and data capabilities that include wireless local area network and internet access as well as a direct-broadcast satellite television capability that permits combatant commanders to conduct business worldwide.

A C-40B cockpit shares the same basic configuration as the C-40A.

Operated by a crew of 11, the C-40B can carry up to 26 passengers in support of global operations. While similar to the US Navy's C-40A, the aircraft features a VIP interior, winglets, and five extended-range fuel tanks. Power is provided by two CFM56-7B27 turbofans each rated at 27,300lb, and its 60,000lb maximum fuel load provides an intercontinental range up to 5,000nm.

As a type, the C-40B was selected to replace the US Air Force's C-137Cs (Boeing 707s) in the Combatant Commander Support Aircraft role, and a contract for the medium lift aircraft was

BELOW • *C-40A BuNo 165836 is based at Naval Air Station North Island, California, assigned to Fleet Logistics Support Squadron 57 (VR-57) 'Conquistadors'.* US NAVY/ RAYMOND RIVARD

awarded in August 2000.

Following first flight in June 2002, the C-40B entered service with the 89th Airlift Wing's 1st Airlift Squadron at Andrews Air Force Base, Maryland, on January 24, 2003. Aircraft serial number 01-0040 was actually delivered to the wing on December 6, 2002 but it completed a 45-day initial operational capability assessment before being declared ready for operations. The Air Force initially purchased three C-40Bs.

Based at Hickam Air Force Base, Hawaii, the 15th Wing's 65th Airlift Squadron accepted the first of two C-40Bs in February 2003. The third C-40B was delivered to the 86th Airlift Wing's 76th Airlift Squadron at Ramstein Air Base, Germany in December 2004.

The fourth and final C-40B was assigned to the 89th Airlift Wing in June 2005. Initially leased, it was purchased in December 2009.

When the C-40Bs assigned to Pacific Air Forces and US Air Forces Europe were returned stateside in 2019, the fleet was consolidated under the 89th Airlift Wing at Andrews Air Force Base, Maryland. As part of that move two C-37As were reassigned from Air Mobility

> Under a $118.6 million contract awarded by the US Navy, AAR Government Services will acquire two Boeing 737-700 (IGW) series aircraft and modify them to the C-40A configuration. The pre-owned 737s will be delivered to Marine Transport Squadron 1 'Roadrunners' by September 2021.

Command to US Air Forces Europe and another went to Pacific Air Forces.

In September 2002, the service agreed to lease up to four C-40 aircraft for a period of seven years and awarded Boeing a $217.7 million contract. Under the agreement, Boeing delivered two pre-owned and one new C-40C aircraft to the District of Columbia Air National Guard's 113th Wing. The wing's 201st Airlift Squadron received two leased B737-7CPs that had previously been operated by Ford Air Services in the United Kingdom, on September 19, 2002. A contract for the aircraft was awarded to Boeing Capital Corporation (BCC Equipment Leasing) earlier on August 6, 2001. The C-40Cs replaced three Boeing 727-100s that had been operated by the squadron under the designation C-22B. A third C-40C (737-7BC) was delivered to the unit in August 2004. The aircraft provide worldwide transportation for the National Guard, Congressional Members/Delegations, Department of Defense Officials, and other government personnel. The aircraft's reconfigurable cabin can accommodate as many as 111 passengers.

The C-40C can carry a full fuel load of 63,000lb and burns it at a rate of about 6,000lb per hour, compared to the C-22B, which carried a maximum fuel load of 56,000lb and burned an average of 10,000lb per hour. With almost double the range of the C-22Bs, the C-40Cs can fly from Washington to Moscow, or from Washington to Hawaii, without requiring a refuelling stop.

The first of four new 737-7DM(WL) aircraft was delivered to the 73rd Airlift Squadron at Scott Air Force Base, Illinois on February 28, 2007. Three additional C-40C aircraft followed in July and November 2007 and November 2011. The unit shares responsibility for the Clippers with the co-located 54th Airlift Squadron, which is an active-duty associate unit assigned to the 375th Air Mobility Wing at Scott.

The initial group of three was ordered in February 2005 and the contract for a fourth leased C-40C was awarded in December 2009. Delivery of the aircraft occurred on November 18, 2011. Air Force Reserve Command C-40Cs have a reconfigurable interior which typically features 40 business-class seats, two work areas with a conference table or divan and accommodations for 11 crew members. Auxiliary fuel tanks extend the aircraft's range to approximately 4,400nm.

Sustainment and modification of the Air Force C-40s is provided by Boeing's Executive Transport Services & Support programme under a seven-year $319 million contract awarded in March 2018.

Beginning in October 2007, Northrop Grumman's AAQ-24(V) Large Aircraft Infrared Countermeasures (LAIRCM) system was installed on the C-40Bs. Another upgrade provided the C-40B and the US Air Force's four C-32A (Boeing 757) aircraft with a common communications suite.

In September 2019, the US Navy awarded Boeing a $15.4 million contract to design and integrate the LAIRCM system on the C-40A.

Installation of the system in the initial Clipper will be completed by the end of 2021.

In April 2017, the 89th Airlift Wing received the first C-40B equipped with an upgraded internet protocol based, open architecture communications network. More recently, Boeing received a contract to upgrade the air force's C-40B and C-40C aircraft to meet the civilian ADS-B mandate, and the US Department of Defense's Mode 5 IFF requirement.

Although production of the 737NG series came to an end with the delivery of C-40A BuNo 169793 to VR-57 in October 2019, Boeing continues to produce a specialised variant based on the -800 series airframe for the US Navy's P-8A Multi-mission Maritime Aircraft (MMA) programme. The Poseidon is currently scheduled to remain in production through late-2023 but any additional sales would extend that date.

E-7A
Wedgetail

Nigel Pittaway outlines the E-7A Wedgetail which has just celebrated ten years of service with the Royal Australian Air Force

In May 2020, the Royal Australian Air Force fleet of Boeing E-7A Wedgetails celebrated 10 years of service, including four and a half years of regular deployments to the Middle East Area of Operations (MEAO).

From a troubled beginning, the airborne early warning and control (AEW&C) aircraft has matured to become what many now regard as the 'AEW&C of choice' on deployments and exercises in Australia and around the world. And a regular series of upgrades are planned to keep it at the cutting edge of technology until at least the early 2030s.

Flown by 2 Squadron Royal Australian Air Force, the Wedgetail first deployed to the Middle East in September 2014 as part of an organic Australian Air Task Group (ATG) under Operation Okra, which also included Boeing F/A-18F Super Hornet strike fighters and a

single Airbus KC-30A multi-role tanker transport. Although the more recent rotations alternated between an E-7A and KC-30A as the coalition air effort drew down, the Wedgetail recorded a mission success rate of around 95% for the four and a half years of operations.

Anecdotally its first mission over Iraq was a solo effort after the coalition Boeing E-3 Sentry it was supposed to be 'shadowing' to gain experience became unserviceable. According to Wedgetail crews this set the scene for the following years and senior Royal Australian Air Force officers deployed to the region have noted it takes three Sentries to fill one line of AEW&C tasking, due to dwindling serviceability rates.

The 14th and final rotation of Royal Australian Air Force Wedgetail crews completed their mission in support of coalition airstrikes in the Middle East

in early February 2019. Speaking on the 10th anniversary of its entry into service, 2 Squadron commanding officer, Wing Commander Jason Brown, said: "In my professional opinion, both the Wedgetail machine and the people who operate it and support it are outstripping other AEW&C capabilities in the world at the present time."

Australia's Wedgetail

Named after an Australian species of Eagle, the Boeing E-7A Wedgetail is a derivative of the commercial 737-700 Increased Gross Weight (IGW)

ABOVE • *E-7A Wedgetail A30-003 departs Andersen Air Force Base, Guam, during the Regional Presence Deployment 2020.* ROYAL AUSTRALIAN AIR FORCE/SGT GUY YOUNG

RIGHT • ROYAL AUSTRALIAN
AIR FORCE/CPL CRAIG
BARRETT

aircraft, with a Northrop Grumman Multi-Role Electronically Scanned Array (MESA) surveillance radar as its primary sensor.

Six aircraft were acquired under Project Air 5077 Phase 3, with selection of the 737/MESA combination made in 1999, beating competing proposals from Lockheed Martin (C-130J Hercules/ APS-145 radar) and Raytheon E-Systems (Airbus A310/Elta radar).

The first two aircraft were converted from a 'green' commercial 737-700IGW (the same baseline aircraft as the initial version of the Boeing Business Jet, or BBJ1) by Boeing in Seattle, but the remainder were modified by Boeing Defence Australia (BDA) at its facility at Royal Australian Air Force Base Amberley in Queensland.

The first aircraft made its maiden flight in the United States in May 2004, but early testing revealed significant deficiencies in radar performance and the Wedgetail had a long and troubled introduction into service, being placed on the Australian Government's defence Projects of Concern list, until solutions were found.

Happily, solutions were indeed found and Wedgetail was removed from the list in 2012, coinciding with the delivery of the final aircraft and the achievement of initial operational capability (IOC).

Just two years later, and before final operational capability (FOC) was declared in May 2015, the Wedgetail was deployed to the Middle East for AEW&C contribution to Operation Okra.

Besides Australia, the 737 AEW&C design is in service with the Türk Hava Kuvvetleri (Turkish Air Force), which purchased four aircraft under the Peace Eagle programme in 2002, and the Republic of Korea Air Force, which ordered four aircraft under the Peace Eye programme in 2006.

More recently the aircraft was being selected by the UK as a replacement for the RAF's ageing Boeing E-3D

Sentry AEW1 aircraft, with Britain's then Defence Secretary Gavin Williamson announcing a decision to acquire five of them on March 22, 2019.

Operation Okra

One Wedgetail departed Australia as part of the Australian ATG in September 2014 and flew its initial mission into Iraqi airspace just a few days after arriving in the United Arab Emirates. By the time that FOC was declared the following May, the Wedgetail had already flown in excess of 100 missions and clocked up 1,200 flying hours in combat.

In November 2015, one aircraft

ABOVE • ROYAL AUSTRALIAN AIR FORCE/CPL SHANNON MCCARTHY

LEFT • *No. 2 Squadron E-7A Wedgetail A30-003 taxis at Elmendorf Air Force Base, Alaska shortly after completing a mission during Exercise Red Flag Alaska 2014-3.* ROYAL AUSTRALIAN AIR FORCE/SGT ANDREW EDDIE

OPPOSITE • *A Royal Australian Air Force E-7A Wedgetail on arrival at a base in the United Arab Emirates.* ROYAL AUSTRALIAN AIR FORCE/CPL DAN PINHORN

set a new record by flying a surveillance and control mission over Syria and Iraq which exceeded 17 hours, due to the unavailability of its E-3 relief aircraft.

Normal missions were around 12 to 13 hours' duration, including the transit into the airspace from and to the Wedgetail's base in the United Arab Emirates, but the mission in question lasted 17.1 hours.

Speaking after the flight, the aircraft captain, who could not be named for security reasons, said: "Our mission on the day was to fly a surveillance pattern over Iraq and Syria to assist coalition strike aircraft to target Islamic State forces on the ground. A mission of this type would normally last around 13 hours, which is quite a long time to be continuously working."

The pilot added: "On this occasion though, as we approached our return time and already well into the night, we were asked to continue on for a few hours longer, so we took on more fuel from a coalition air to air refuelling aircraft and kept flying. It wasn't until we landed that I realised I had hit the 17.1-hour mark, a record for the E-7A."

As the new kid on the block, Wedgetail's presence is often

The Australian government has an E-7A recapitalisation plan, known as Project Air 7001, with up to AUD 21.1 billion forecast in the Australian government's 2020 Force Structure Plan for a replacement. However, this project is not due to begin until at least 2029.

requested at high-end air combat exercises such as the US Red Flag series, as word of its utility spreads. The aircraft is also a regular participant in Australia's biennial Pitch Black air combat exercise and, during the most recent iteration in July and August 2018, the writer spoke with 2 Squadron personnel about their experiences, including senior engineering officer, Squadron Leader Shane Taylor, who provided details of the aircraft's performance in the MEAO at that time.

Sqn Ldr Taylor said: "By some margin, the Wedgetail provides a world-leading, a genuinely global-class, AEW&C platform. We've been supporting Okra for a little over four years now and really fighting a good fight over there."

He added: "The Wedgetail is an AEW&C surveillance platform, essentially it is the eyes and ears of the air war. It's about providing the best situational awareness that you can in a high-end fifth generation war fight. We have a number of very experienced mission controllers and mission commanders in the back of the aircraft and it's their job to ensure that all of the various players in the airspace are force-marshalled in a safe fashion and maintain appropriate separation distances."

Exercise Pitch Black 2018

The Royal Australian Air Force's six Wedgetail aircraft are based at Royal Australian Air Force Williamtown, north of Sydney and home to most of the air force's tactical fighter fleet, but regular deployments are made to Royal Australian Air Force Base Tindal in the Northern Territory, where 2 Squadron

maintains facilities, including a shelter able to accommodate two aircraft.

One Wedgetail was deployed to Tindal for the duration of Pitch Black, and during the large force employment phase of the exercise, where Surveillance and Control Officer (SCO) Flying Officer Brodie Jones described a typical mission.

Jones said: "The ten operator consoles are all the same, so everyone will sit in a certain way, depending on what we're doing. We generally carry one or two electronic support measures operators, who are ex-P-3 Orion maritime crew members, and they will analyse signals for the detection of threats such as surface-to-air-missiles or enemy fighters. The job we do is surveillance and battle management, so we tie all the assets in the airspace together and pass information out to them."

Flying Officer Jones explained that the E-7A's typical operating altitude is 31,000 feet, where optimal radar performance is obtained. He said that the Wedgetail will be generally established in long orbits, which utilise the larger, much more powerful, side arrays of the MESA radar to the maximum amount possible, giving a radar horizon of just over 215 nautical miles.

He explained: "We carry two or three

pilots – if it's a longer flight we'll take three, so we can swap one out every now and then. Down the back we have the mission commander, who is the liaison between the front [flight deck] and back ends and he's in charge of the whole mission.

"Then down from him, the systems officer is responsible for the operation of the radar and all our communications and datalinks, making sure they are running as they're supposed to. Next, there's the senior controller who looks after the team of surveillance and

control officers, including myself. He is responsible for liaising with other agencies, air traffic control and ground control agencies, such as the air force's Mobile Control and Reporting Unit (114 MCRU) here at Pitch Black, and also for the product that the SCOs are putting off the aircraft."

For Operation Okra, Jones explained that the Wedgetail was allocated a sector of airspace, within which it was also responsible for checking other airborne assets in and out of the area and managing the rapidly-changing (air ✈

to air refuelling) tanker plan, but the Pitch Black mission set was more traditional.

He said: "We are performing the general command and control and battle management piece, where the general role is fighter control – detecting the enemy's disposition and passing out directions from (exercise referees) White Force about how they want the exercise to run and what learning outcomes they want to achieve."

During Pitch Black 18 the Wedgetail was operating for the attacking

Blue Force, alongside a Gulfstream G550CAEW from the Republic of Singapore Air Force's 111 Squadron. Flg Off Jones continued: "Most of the Red Air control is done by the ground control agencies during this exercise, and our mission sets are largely centred around Offensive Counter Air (OCA). We'll generally split the airspace up into two lanes, because there's a lot of airspace out there to actually run in, so we'll generally take one and the Singaporeans will take the other, but

we might also divide the duties and they might take a force-marshalling role, for example.

"The scope of this exercise is the biggest training outcome for us and the different international partner we're working with, you just can't get that training anywhere else, where there are up to 100 jets airborne. I just don't think you can compare to it, there's that much talking going on and that much stuff being thrown around, it's hard to keep track of."

OPPOSITE • *E-7A Wedgetail A30-001 receives fuel during a mission flown from the United Arab Emirates in support of Operation Okra.* ROYAL AUSTRALIAN AIR FORCE/CPL BRENTON KWATERSKI

BELOW • *Ground maintenance crew prepare an E-7A Wedgetail for a mission from the main logistics base in the Middle East.* ROYAL AUSTRALIAN AIR FORCE/CPL BRENTON KWATERSKI

In May 2020, the Royal Australian Air Force fleet of Boeing E-7A Wedgetails celebrated 10 years of service, including four and a half years of regular deployments to the Middle East Area of Operations.

Future of Wedgetail

Boeing Defence Australia has been rolling out an incremental series of upgrades under Project Air 5077 Phase 5A, largely to improve interoperability and compliance, but also to address some obsolescence issues.

Systems to be added include a Traffic Collision Avoidance System, IFF Mode 5 and minor upgrades to the MESA radar. The first software release, Release 0.5, was rolled out to the fleet in 2018 and followed by Release 1.0 in 2019. A further increment, known as Release 2.0, will add further capability, including a wideband satellite communications (SATCOM) system to increase the flow of data able to be sent and received during a mission.

Scott Carpendale, BDA's vice president and managing director, explained: "We're also doing some other upgrades, such as changing the displays in the operator consoles from a single display to a dual unit and integrating capabilities that we've previously added to the aircraft, such as IP chat, into the display rather than having a separate display. In addition, we're doing some mission computing upgrades to take advantage of the increased data throughput that Wideband SATCOM and other solutions provide."

Further into the future, Project Air 5077 Phase 6 will be a comprehensive mid-life upgrade of the Wedgetail, but that is still some time away. Carpendale said: "The Australian government is going through their definition and approval processes and we'll then get some direction as to what capabilities they want to include on the platform. We've already given them some support, in terms of providing different option sets, but we're waiting for the Commonwealth to give us some guidance on the boundaries of the programme."

While Phase 6 will be an upgrade and not a replacement of Wedgetail, the Australian government has an E-7A recapitalisation plan, known as Project Air 7001, with up to AUD 21.1 billion forecast in the Australian government's 2020 Force Structure Plan for a replacement. However, this project is not due to begin until at least 2029 and Wedgetail is set to remain a familiar sight in Australian skies for years to come.

The first P-8A Poseidon delivered to the US Navy fleet arrived at Naval Air Station Jacksonville, Florida in March 2012. That aircraft was assigned to Patrol Squadron 30 (VP-30) 'Pro's Nest'. As the Fleet Replacement Squadron, VP-30 has responsibility for training all P-8 aviators and mission crew, not just from the US Navy but also Foreign Military Sale (FMS) customers. Australia,

the UK, and Norway are examples.

Naval Air Systems Command (NAVAIR) is the contracting authority for all P-8A Poseidon aircraft, which are managed by PMA-290, the Maritime Patrol and Reconnaissance Aircraft programme office based at Naval Air Station Patuxent River, Maryland. One of its tasks is to ensure all allied P-8As share the same baseline configuration as the US Navy's aircraft.

Commonality of FMS aircraft enables interoperability and allows all aircraft to undergo forward fit of sub-systems on the assembly lines run by Boeing Commercial Airplanes at Renton and Boeing Defense Systems at King County Airport both near Seattle in Washington.

In fact, the P-8 is the first US Navy combat aircraft built from the ground up on a mature and efficient commercial aircraft assembly line. That's beneficial

All-out Sub Hunter

Mark Ayton provides an overview of the US Navy's maritime surveillance aircraft, the Boeing P-8A Poseidon

ABOVE • *P-8A Poseidon test aircraft BuNo 167954 is one of five in operation with Air Test and Evaluation Squadron 20 (VX-20) based at Naval Air Station Patuxent River, Maryland.* NAVAL AIR SYSTEMS COMMAND/PMA-290

because it makes the production process more cost effective. Since the initial contract award back in 2009, PMA-290 has reduced costs by more than 30%, which has saved the US Navy more than $2.2 billion across the programme.

So, what is a P-8A Poseidon? Put simply, a military version of the Boeing 737, though a highly modified variant. Every P-8 is in fact a hybrid comprising a 737-800 fuselage and a 737-900 wing,

major components selected by Boeing's design team to enable the aircraft to meet the US Navy's requirements for the maritime surveillance role, which includes anti-submarine warfare (ASW).

According to official US Department of Defense documents, to meet the requirements, the P-8A incorporates an integrated sensor suite that includes radar, electro-optical and electronic signal detection systems

to detect, identify, locate, and track surface targets. An integrated acoustic sonobuoy launch and monitoring system detects, identifies, locates, and tracks submarine targets. Sensor systems also provide tactical situational awareness information for dissemination to fleet forces and intelligence, surveillance, and reconnaissance (ISR) information for exploitation by joint intelligence agencies.

JET

DANGER →

INTAKE

ABOVE • *Full colour tail markings featuring a Pelican applied to P-8A BuNo 168434. The aircraft is assigned to Patrol Squadron 45 (VP-45) 'Pelicans', the third fleet squadron to transition from the P-3C Orion to the P-8A Poseidon.* US NAVY/VP-45

OPPOSITE • *A Royal Australian Air Force No.11 Squadron P-8A Poseidon loaded with an inert ATK-84J Harpoon training missile during a training sortie over the Southern Ocean.* ROYAL AUSTRALIAN AIR FORCE/CPL CRAIG BARRETT

Aircraft are fitted with a directed infrared countermeasure system to improve survivability against infrared missile threats, and fuel tank inerting and fire protection systems to reduce aircraft vulnerability.

Aircraft Configurations

During the P-8 programme's System Development and Demonstration phase, NAVAIR's five test aircraft were configured to Increment 1 standard featuring an APY-10 radar, and three mission critical systems: acoustic, ALQ-240 electronic support measures (ESM) and an MX-20 HD EO/IR for imaging and targeting. Surface radar tracking, sensor display and track management, sensor bias correction, sensor control and mission replay are all baseline capabilities.

In accordance with the P-8's spiral development the next phase of capabilities dubbed Increment 2 (previously called Spiral 1) was integrated through Engineering Change Proposals (ECPs).

ECP 1 added the Multi-static Active Coherent (MAC) wide area sonar system used to search for and locate threat submarines. The MAC system comprises source and receiver sonobuoys, acoustic processing, and a mission computer software suite. Early MAC capability was introduced in FY2015, followed by release of the full MAC version in 2017.

Other features included the

Automatic Identification System (AIS), HAAWC torpedo and sensors, rapid capability insertion, and updates to the tactical operations centre housed in the aft cabin.

ECP 2 included two new receivers for the AIS, and new algorithms to the MAC and the AIS operator interface which offer noise reduction, and therefore greater probability of submarine detection.

Operational flight testing of ECP 2 finished in December 2017 and certificated, as operationally effective a host of modifications including receiver aerial refuelling, advanced employment modes of the Block 1C AGM-84D Harpoon air-launched, day/night, adverse weather, over-the-horizon precision strike missile, and multiple communication system upgrades.

In contrast, and despite significant efforts to improve the P-8's sensors, operational testing deemed overall ISR capabilities to be limited because of persistent performance shortfalls. PMA-290 confirmed that where deficiencies initially existed, work continues to resolve the problems and implement corrections into aircraft already delivered to the fleet and all future deliveries.

In an attempt to continuously improve P-8 ASW capabilities, NAVAIR has tested, in under water acoustic terms, a higher source-level active sonobuoy, and combined it with new tactics, and improvements to the MAC software.

AGM-158C Long-Range Anti-Ship Missile

The AGM-158C is part of a US Navy acquisition programme to meet the near term capability gap for a flexible, long-range, advanced, anti-surface weapon for use against maritime targets. As such the Long Range Anti-Ship Missile (LRASM) programme office is developing the missile as the initial increment of the Offensive Anti-Surface Warfare (OASuW) system for open ocean and littoral strikes from an extended range.

Designated the AGM-158C, the LRASM is a 14ft (4.26m) long subsonic, long range, precision-guided anti-ship standoff missile weighing 2,100lb (953kg). Its design and form are based on the AGM-158B Joint Air-to-Surface Standoff Missile-Extended Range (JASSM-ER).

According to Lockheed Martin Missiles and Fire Control Strike Weapons, the LRASM features:

- 1,000lb (454kg) penetrator and blast fragmentation warhead

- infrared day/night, all-weather capable precision routing and guidance system

- 200nm (370km) guidance range from the launch aircraft

- multi-modal radio frequency sensor suite

- new datalink used for receiving target updates

- new altimeter

- uprated power system

- digital anti-jam GPS navigation system

Lockheed Martin claims the missile will be able to detect and destroy specific targets underway at sea by flying toward an initial point at medium altitude before descending to a low altitude, skimming the ocean surface during the terminal phase of its flight, guided by its on board sensors.

Once the new sonobuoy is fielded, re-evaluation of the MAC capability is anticipated to measure performance improvements.

ECP 3 featured additional upgrades to the MAC and HAAWC systems, and began fielding in 2017, a process that is expected to be complete in the coming year.

In April 2016, the under-secretary of defense for acquisition, technology and logistics approved a revised P-8 acquisition strategy that incorporated all of the Increment 3 (previously called Spiral 2) enhanced capabilities ✈

into the baseline P-8A programme. Consequently, all capabilities are now developed and delivered as a series of ECPs, which incrementally increase combat capability as the technologies mature. Those included in Increment 3 are ECP 4, ECP 5, ECP 6, and ECP 7.

ECP 4 comprises upgrades to the demand-assigned multiple access UHF satellite communication integrated waveform dubbed DAMA, and the aircraft's targeting capability.

ECP 5 includes Link-16 messaging for net-enabled weapons, third party targeting, and electronic warfare coordination, high frequency radio internet protocol, a new integrated broadcast service (IBS) receiver, IBS filtering, and integration of the upgraded, network-capable AGM-84N Harpoon II+ anti-ship missile. An upgrade of the Block 1C featuring an improved GPS guidance kit and a datalink to enable the missile to receive in-flight targeting updates.

ECP 6 incorporates a new open system architecture, ASW signals intelligence, improvements to the combat system's ability to process and display classified information, wideband SATCOM, and a software upgrade of the Minotaur track management and mission management system. Minotaur disseminates and correlates data fed from various sensors into a comprehensive battlespace picture, and via the network, shares the information with other aircraft and vessels.

ECP 7 incorporates enhanced MAC capabilities via the combat system architecture.

Components of ECP 6 and ECP 7 are currently in various stages of development and are scheduled for initial release to the fleet in FY2025.

Fleet aircraft are currently being delivered in an ECP 5 configuration, with a retrofit programme of fielded aircraft in progress to maintain commonality across the Fleet.

The HAAWC torpedo has one more operational test period scheduled for 2020. Provided the weapon is deemed operationally effective by the Operational Test and Evaluation Force, NAVAIR expects to field HAAWC before the end of 2020.

Weapons

P-8s are currently cleared to carry two kinetic weapons, the standard Mk54 torpedo and the Block 1C AGM-84D Harpoon all-weather, over-the-horizon, anti-ship missile.

The Mk54 torpedo is the US Navy's primary ASW weapon. It combines the sonar transceiver of the Mk50 torpedo with the legacy warhead and propulsion system of the older Mk46; both types convert to Mk54 via an upgrade kit. The baseline standard is designated Mod 0, the first modification is Mod 1 comprising an upgrade of the torpedo's sonar array with a new 112-element hydrophone front end (from 52 elements), and new processors providing higher resolution. Associated software upgrades are designed to exploit these features to improve target detection and enhance false target rejection as well as correct previously identified deficiencies.

The standard Mk54 torpedo is also being upgraded to one capable of high altitude launch with the HAAWC or (High Altitude Anti-submarine warfare Weapon Capability). HAAWC is an independently procured adapter kit comprising wings, a tail and a GPS-guidance section interfaced to the aircraft. The kit permits long-range, high-altitude, GPS-guided deployment of the torpedo by a P-8A aircraft.

A follow-on capability to receive in-flight targeting updates via Link-16 from the P-8A is expected to be added in a later programme phase. In-flight updates will not be available in the baseline HAAWC kit.

BELOW • *An ATM-84A captive carriage Harpoon missile with dozens of reference marks applied for photogrammetry during a store separation test. Photogrammetry is a technique for collection of quantitative data from cameras mounted on the aircraft, used to validate the models developed in the store separation tests.* NAVAL AIR SYSTEMS COMMAND/PMA-290

AGM-84D Harpoon II Anti-Ship Missile

Harpoon II is an all-weather, over-the-horizon, anti-ship missile system which is effective against moving or stationary surface ships ranging in size from patrol boats to large vessels.

Harpoon uses a turbojet sustainer engine to fly a low-level cruise trajectory followed by a sea-skimming terminal phase. It has the ability to execute a pop-up manoeuvre just before impact to counter close in defences and to enhance the 500lb (227kg) warhead's penetration.

The 12ft 6in (3.83m) long, 1,160lb (525kg) missile uses a new GPS-aided inertial navigation system (which replaces the original INS mid-course system) and active radar guidance, and a net-enabled datalink used for in-flight target updates.

Boeing claims the upgraded missile offers ten times better capability compared to the older Block IC.

The first P-8A Poseidon delivered to the US Navy fleet arrived at Naval Air Station Jacksonville, Florida in March 2012. That aircraft was assigned to Patrol Squadron 30 (VP-30) 'Pro's Nest'. As the Fleet Replacement Squadron, VP-30 has responsibility for training all P-8 aviators and mission crew, not just from the US Navy but also Foreign Military Sale customers.

RIGHT • *An aircrewman operator loads a sonobuoy on to a storage rack aboard a P-8A Poseidon.* US NAVY/ MASS COMMUNICATION SPECIALIST SEAMAN THOMAS HIGGINS

In May 2019, NAVAIR's Air Test and Evaluation Squadron 20 (VX-20), the P-8 developmental test unit released five HAAWCs from a P-8A. Four were Mk54 test articles used to assess delivery accuracy. The fifth was configured at Mod 0 standard and used to determine both the delivery accuracy, and reliability. Results of the five releases proved that HAAWC meets the required level of performance.

The Block 1C AGM-84D Harpoon can be employed against moving and stationary surface ships of various classes. It has the capability to cruise just above the surface toward its target, and during the terminal phase execute a pop-up manoeuvre to counter close-in ship defences and to enhance the warhead's penetration.

PMA-290 is currently completing the initial contracting effort for integration of the precision-guided AGM-158C Long Range Anti-Ship Missile (LRASM) on the P-8A Poseidon. Complex sub-systems include a low probability of intercept radar, an infrared imaging sensor, a data link, passive RF, and threat warning receivers. Coupled with INS/GPS navigation and artificial intelligence (AI) software, all tied to the autopilot and flight management system, it makes for a capable weapon.

In fact, the AI software provides automatic dissemination of data fed from the radar and ESM sensors enable identification and geolocation of threat emissions. That same AI software then determines a route to target which harbours the least number and array of threats. Additional battle space data is fed via the data link from off-board sensors.

According to an official US government contract opportunity notice, PMA-290 is soliciting information from industry to determine potential contractors who have the skills, experience and knowledge

Mk54 Lightweight Torpedo

The Mk54 is the latest variant of the Mk46 torpedo deployed to detect and attack underwater targets in deep water and littoral environments.

Processing algorithms allow the Mk54 to analyse information, edit out false targets or countermeasures, and pursue identified threats.

The Mk54 torpedo uses the warhead and propulsion subsystems from the Mk46, and the latest systems integrated on the Mk50 and the advanced capability version of the heavyweight Mk48.

Incremental improvements to the Mk54 are planned. The first, dubbed Mod 1, includes a new higher resolution sonar array and software.

LEFT • *A standard Mk54 torpedo fitted with a High Altitude Anti-submarine warfare Weapon Capability air launch accessory kit* LOCKHEED MARTIN

required to perform aeromechanical and software integration of the LRASM onto the P-8A aircraft. The contract is likely to run between January 2021 and January 2026.

The notice also states the potential to include, but not limited to, additional weapon systems including 500lb, 1,000lb and 2,000lb-class variants of the Joint Direct Attack Munition, Mk62, Mk63 and Mk65 mines, GBU-53/B Small Diameter Bomb II, Miniature Air Launched Decoy, BRU-55 bomb rack, and the Universal Armament Interface.

PMA-290 confirmed that industry sources are looking at other weapon options, but the LRASM is the only one currently being pursued by NAVAIR.

Mission Employment

Fleet squadrons generally operate the P-8 aircraft in a similar way to their previous mount the P-3 Orion, but there are differences. The Poseidon is not

equipped with a magnetic anomaly detector; a system that requires the aircraft to fly at low-level for good effect.

Determined by a mix of weather, cloud cover and which of its sensors are required to meet the mission requirements, the Poseidon generally operates at higher altitudes.

Operating differences between the straight wing, propeller-driven P-3C Orion and the swept wing P-8A

Poseidon initially created concern for crews transitioning to the Boeing jet. According to former PMA-290 programme manager, Captain Rossi: "The higher airspeed means a slightly higher turn radius, but because the autopilot is coupled into the mission system, and the autopilot is functional, very reliable and gives the operator the ability to get ahead of the aircraft [in terms of the mission plan], the

integration and automation mitigates the higher turn radius.

"One operating aspect of the P-3 was the amount of high-angle bank manoeuvre, which required a lot of movement of the power lever and the controls to quickly turn around to get back to where the sonobuoy drop was missed. Thanks to the integration and automation on the P-8, the operator can get much further ahead of the aircraft that the crew does not run into such a situation and are therefore not required to do many of the things required in a P-3. Flying a little higher and a little faster more than makes-up for that."

The modern, well-equipped P-8 offers its crew a level of automation unmatched by the earlier era P-3C Orion. Lt Cdr Will Noose, a NAVAIR P-8 test pilot compared an example of the Poseidon's flight deck automation with the P-3. "When a TACCO [a tactical coordinator] on a P-3 wants a certain sonobuoy pattern in the water, he or she places a picture of the pattern on the display for the pilots to manually fly to the right points in the air from which to drop the sonobuoys. If the aircraft is close enough to those points, the system will automatically drop.

"The P-8's robust navigation system is tied to the mission system, which allows the pilot to switch into a tactical

"The P-8A Poseidon is proving itself in the anti-submarine warfare, maritime security operation and ISR roles. The Navy fleet has passed 250,000 flight hours, the 100th US Navy aircraft was delivered to VP-30 at Jacksonville on May 14, 2020 and aircraft production currently continues through 2023." Captain Eric Gardner, PMA-290's program manager for maritime patrol and reconnaissance aircraft

mode that allows the TACCO to control the lateral navigation of the aircraft. So, when a tactic is placed on the screen to lay a pattern of sonobuoys, or to set up and orbit, the TACCO can set that up and essentially get control of the aircraft's lateral navigation from the back end and can fly the aircraft without lots of explanation and drawing of pictures. In this sense we have leveraged the automation already built into the aircraft to accomplish the mission."

The P-8's navigation system allows the flight crew to create a flight plan, dubbed the magenta line, and enables the aircraft to fly to the middle of an ocean, stay on station and return to base.

By applying GPS approach capability to a tactical situation, the navigation system ensures sonobuoy drops are not missed, and through automation offloads some of the pilots flying inputs (they continue to monitor) enabling them to concentrate on the tactical picture and stay farther ahead in the mission plan.

Sonobuoys, weapon bay doors, the EO/IR turret, and the authorisation

transfer that allows the TACCO to launch a weapon are all commanded from a control panel located on the lower aft centre console. Pilots hold ultimate launch and veto authority, though the TACCO actually launches the weapon because he or she has more situational awareness when tracking either a submarine or a target, and can better control targeting.

Current P-8s are fitted with five commonly-configured operator workstations, but work is ongoing to increase the number to six. Each workstation has a 27-inch (685mm) touch screen which can be configured with different portals to suit the operator's personal set-up preference.

When fitted with a joystick, a workstation provides the operator with the ability to control the MX-20 EO/IR turret. Alternatively, the operator can control the turret using a particular pull-up display menu and the track ball.

The Poseidon's collective computer processing capacity is much greater than that of a P-3 which affords mission crew operators more ways to manipulate

P-8 Poseidon orders and production lots

Order date	Lot	Quantity	Customer
July 2004	Test aircraft including one for ground test	6	6 US Navy
January 2009		8	8 DCS/India
January 2011	LRIP Lot 1	6	6 US Navy
November 2011	LRIP Lot 2	7	7 US Navy
September 2012	LRIP Lot 3	11	11 US Navy
July 2013	LRIP Lot 4	13	13 US Navy
February 2014	FRP Lot 5	16	16 US Navy
August 2015	FRP Lot 6	13	9 US Navy 4 FMS/RAAF
January 2016	FRP Lot 7	22	18 US Navy 4 FMS/RAAF
July 2016		4	4 DCS/India
March 2017	FRP Lot 8	17	11 US Navy 4 FMS/RAAF 2 FMS/RAF
December 2017	FRP Lot 9	10	7 US Navy 3 FMS/RAF
May 2018	FRP Lot 9 addition	3	3 US Navy
January 2019	FRP Lot 10	19	10 US Navy 5 FMS/KNL 4 FMS/RAF
December 2019		9	9 DCS/India
March 2020	FRP Lot 11	18	8 US Navy 6 FMS/RoKN 4 FMS/RNZAF
Total		**182**	**119 US Navy** **18 DCS** **45 FMS**

the data acquired and extract more information from the data.

An Orion mission crew uses two plots. One displays lines, the second shows energy and its frequency. Both plots are used to determine noise in the water though the system lacks capability to overlay the two plots particularly well. Consequently, the operator must manually interpret the plots.

The process is automated on a P-8. Both plots are overlaid on a topological map so the energy intensity can be seen allowing the operator to extract and interpret more information and in a different way.

Once the TACCO has selected a drop pattern details are passed to the flight deck, the request is entered in to the flight management computer, autopilot flies the pattern and active and passive sonobuoys are launched automatically.

Launching is more of a manual process on a P-3C, which can carry 84 sonobuoys and passively process 32 at a time; a P-8 can carry 129 and passively process 64 at a time.

Sonobuoy stowage racks are located toward the aft end of the cabin close to the six launchers of which there are two types. Three sonobuoy rotary launchers (SLRs) designated X, Y and Z each holding ten buoys, and three single-shot launchers designated 1, 2 and 3. When fully loaded, the TACCO has an arsenal of 33 sonobuoys ready for launch, a process more automated on the P-8 compared to the P-3.

Poseidon Transition

VP-30 played an integral part in managing the Navy's squadron-by-squadron transition from the legendary P-3C Orion to the P-8A Poseidon. As each Navy patrol squadron entered transition training, its crews spent six months learning to fly the aircraft and a subsequent 12-month fleet readiness training plan learning to operate it effectively and tactically.

Patrol Squadron 16 (VP-16) 'Eagles' was the first operational Poseidon unit to have the honour of making the type's initial operational capability (IOC) in 2013.

According to the then Commanding Officer of VP-16, Captain Dan Papp: "The P-8A exceeded P-3 performance in mission completion rate, on-time take-off rate, number of in-flight aborts and persistence at range. The aircraft proved to be a game-changer for theatre ASW in the Western Pacific, due to its increased range and endurance, higher dash speed to get to the area of action faster and larger passive search area, due to its capability to process 64 versus 32 sonobuoys. Additionally, the P-8's acoustic processor demonstrated better reliability and longer passive detection ranges than a P-3."

Capt Papp added that the ALQ-240 ESM system significantly extended the tactical surveillance range of the P-8A and enabled aircrews to quickly locate surface contacts of interest in the dense maritime environment of the western Pacific. Papp also explained how the data link and sensor fusion capability of the P-8 enhanced aircrew situational awareness and enabled higher-fidelity tactical reporting to operational commanders.

On May 15, 2020, Patrol Squadron 40 (VP-40) 'Fighting Marlins' was designated safe-for-flight, an event that concluded the US Navy's fleet transition to the P-8 Poseidon.

Summarising the programme's milestones to date, Captain Eric Gardner, PMA-290's program manager for maritime patrol and reconnaissance aircraft said: "The P-8A Poseidon is proving itself in the anti-submarine warfare, maritime security operation and ISR roles. The Navy fleet has passed 250,000 flight hours, the 100th US Navy aircraft was delivered to VP-30 at Jacksonville on May 14 and aircraft production currently continues through 2023."

> The standard Mk54 torpedo is also being upgraded to one capable of high altitude launch with the High Altitude Anti-submarine warfare Weapon Capability, an independently procured adapter kit comprising wings, a tail and a GPS-guidance section interfaced to the aircraft. The kit permits long-range, high-altitude, GPS-guided deployment of the torpedo by a P-8A aircraft.

BELOW • *A RAAF P-8A Poseidon supports sea trials for the HMAS Hobart in the Gulf St Vincent off the coast of Adelaide, Australia.* ROYAL AUSTRALIAN AIR FORCE/CPL CRAIG BARRETT